FIGHTING WORDS

FIGHTING WORDS

. . . .

Writers Lambast Other Writers

. . . .

—From Aristotle to Anne Rice

. . . .

JAMES CHARLTON, editor

✸

ILLUSTRATIONS BY TULLIO PERICOLI

1994

ALGONQUIN BOOKS OF CHAPEL HILL

Published by
Algonquin Books of Chapel Hill
Post Office Box 2225
Chapel Hill, North Carolina 27515-2225

a division of
WORKMAN PUBLISHING COMPANY, INC.
708 Broadway
New York, New York 10003

LIBRARY OF CONGRESS CATALOGING-IN-PUBLICATION DATA
Fighting Words: Writers Lambast Other Writers—From Aristotle
to Anne Rice / edited by James Charlton.—1st ed.

p. cm.
Includes index.
ISBN 1-56512-073-6
1. Authorship—Quotations, maxims, etc. 2. Authors—Quotations.
I. Charlton, James. 1939-
PN165. F54 1994
808.88'2—dc20   94-1988
CIP

10 9 8 7 6 5 4 3 2 1
First Edition

I prefer dead writers because you don't run into them at parties.

FRAN LEBOWITZ

. . . .

Dead or alive, writers are among my favorite people. I enjoy their company, their opinions and views, their fascination with words and ideas. It is a solitary profession they've chosen, and I respect the difficulties of having to face a blank page (or nowadays, a blank screen) each morning and hope that the literary muse will stop by and whisper in their ear.

It is curious, though, to hear writers whispering among themselves, be it at a publication party, a literary conference, or the Lion's Head. The *obiter dictum* is occasionally literary—subjects like plot, phrasing, construction are discussed—but mostly it has to do with personalities. Get two authors together and they'll talk about a third; worse yet, they'll castigate publishers or compare advances. Any good writer is jealous of another's ability with words or output, envious of a better review or a stack of the other writer's newest title in the window of a local bookstore. Oh, writers do mouth the correct pieties about another's latest publication, but too often this sort of literary logrolling is done at the behest of an agent or editor they share in common. The praise is weak, pale, insipid at best, and rarely sincere. Venom and rebuke—that's what comes from the heart.

My theory is that writers don't much like each other. Nor can they—their relationships with each other are too complicated. I can't understand how two writers can be married to each other any more than I can fathom how two actors can be. It seems to me that the more contact writers have with other writers, the more vitriolic they are on the subject of one another. If a writer is only known from afar, through his or her written word or an occasional meeting at a writers' conference, the observations about that person are more restrained. It is daily contact, like stone rubbing stone, that most often produces sparks. London in the eighteenth and nineteenth centuries, Paris in the 1920s, Greenwich Village in the 1950s—here, where the writers drank and ate together, argued, compared notes and drafts, is where the barbs are sharpest. Familiarity *does* indeed breed contempt—as well as some great and memorable quotations.

In *Fighting Words,* I've gathered the best of these nosegays and nose-thumbings. It was a labor of love and respect. I hope every writer and book lover will enjoy reading them.

JAMES CHARLTON
New York City

Failure is inevitable for the writer. Any writer. I don't care who he is, or how great he is, or what he's written. Sooner or later he's going to flop and everybody who admired him will try to write him off as a bum. He can't help it. He's bound to write something bad. Shakespeare wrote a few bad plays. Tolstoy was turning out some pretty dreadful stuff at the end of his life. Name me one great writer who hasn't had some failure.

IRWIN SHAW

A cliché anthologist . . . and maker of ragamuffin manikins.

ARISTOPHANES, on Euripides

❋

The more I read him, the less I wonder that they poisoned him.

THOMAS BABINGTON MACAULAY, on Socrates

❋

His decision was not to abandon his principles, but rather give his life to prove a point. I am not quite as fearless about dying and will, after an untoward noise such as a car backfiring, leap directly into the arms of the person I am conversing with.

WOODY ALLEN, on Socrates

❋

Aristotle invented science, but destroyed philosophy.

ALFRED NORTH WHITEHEAD, on Aristotle

❋

Aristotle was famous for knowing everything. He taught that the brain exists merely to cool the blood and is not involved in the process of thinking. This is true only of certain persons.

WILL CUPPY, on Aristotle

Aristotle could have avoided the mistake of thinking that women have fewer teeth than men by the simple device of asking Mrs. Aristotle to open her mouth.

BERTRAND RUSSELL, on Aristotle

❋

I strive to be brief, and I become obscure.   HORACE, on himself

❋

Virgil's great judgement appears in putting things together, and in his picking gold out of the dunghills of old Roman writers.

ALEXANDER POPE, on Virgil

❋

As great a poet as Dante might have been, I wouldn't have had the slightest wish to have known him personally. He was a terrible prima donna.   W. H. AUDEN, on Dante

❋

A hyena that wrote poetry in tombs.

HORACE WALPOLE, on Dante

❋

Chaucer, notwithstanding the praises bestowed on him, I think obscene and contemptible: he owes his celebrity merely to antiquity.   LORD BYRON, on Geoffrey Chaucer

Dante

He was a staunch churchman, but he laughed at priests. He was an able public servant and courtier, but his views upon sexual morality were extremely lax. He sympathized with poverty, but did nothing to improve the lot of the poor. . . . And yet, as we read him, we are absorbing morality at every pore.

VIRGINIA WOOLF, on Geoffrey Chaucer

❀

Casting my mind's eye over the whole of fiction, the only absolutely original creation that I can think of is *Don Quixote*.

SOMERSET MAUGHAM, on Miguel de Cervantes

❀

Donne had no imagination, but as much wit, I think, as any writer can possibly have.

ALEXANDER POPE, on John Donne

❀

Dr. Donne's verses are like the peace of God; they pass all understanding.

JAMES I, on John Donne

❀

There are people who cannot taste olives—and I cannot much relish Ben Jonson, though I have taken some pains to do it, and went to the task with every sort of good will. I do not deny his power or his merit; far from it: but it is to me of a repulsive and unamiable kind.

WILLIAM HAZLITT, on Ben Jonson

He was not only a professed imitator of Horace, but a learned plagiary of all the others; you track him everywhere in their snow.   JOHN DRYDEN, on Ben Jonson

❈

Reading him is like wading through glue.
                    ALFRED, LORD TENNYSON, on Ben Jonson

❈

I remember, the Players have often mentioned it as an honour to Shakespeare, that in his writing, (whatsoever he penned) he never blotted out a line. My answer hath been, would he had blotted a thousand.

                    BEN JONSON, on William Shakespeare

❈

We don't all dig Shakespeare uniformly, or even *Little Red Riding Hood.*   RALPH ELLISON, on William Shakespeare

❈

With the single exception of Homer, there is no eminent writer, not even Sir Walter Scott, whom I despise so entirely as I despise Shakespeare.
                    GEORGE BERNARD SHAW, on William Shakespeare

The undisputed fame enjoyed by Shakespeare as a writer . . . is, like every other lie, a great evil.

> LEO TOLSTOY, on William Shakespeare

❋

There were occasions when Shakespeare was a very bad writer indeed. You can see how often in books of quotations. People who like quotations love meaningless generalizations.

> GRAHAM GREENE, on William Shakespeare

❋

I'll bet Shakespeare compromised himself a lot; anybody who's in the entertainment industry does to some extent.

> CHRISTOPHER ISHERWOOD, on William Shakespeare

❋

Think of the Bible and Homer, think of Shakespeare and think of me.

> GERTRUDE STEIN, on herself

❋

Because in a previous lifetime that's who I was.

> JACK KEROUAC, on why he understood Shakespeare

❋

Shakespeare is in the singular fortunate position of being, to all intents and purposes, anonymous.

> W. H. AUDEN, on William Shakespeare

He thought woman made only for obedience, and man only for rebellion.   SAMUEL JOHNSON, on John Milton

❁

Milton seems to the colleges profound because he wrote of hell, a great place, and is dead.
                    STEPHEN LEACOCK, on John Milton

❁

His fame is gone out like a candle in a snuff and his memory will always stink.   WILLIAM WINSTANLEY, on John Milton

❁

If length be considered a merit, it hath no other.
          EDMUND WALLER, on John Milton's *Paradise Lost*

❁

Think of *Robinson Crusoe* or *Journal of the Plague Year*. The things Defoe was doing—mixing fact and fiction—are really as disreputable and irresponsible as anything any of us have done since.
                    E. L. DOCTOROW, on Daniel Defoe

❁

With the one exception of his Moll, all Defoe's characters are completely invisible and utterly, not so much dead, as unalive in the sense that tailors' dummies are unalive.
                    FORD MADOX FORD, on Daniel Defoe

Swift has a higher reputation than he deserves. His excellence is strong sense; for his humour, though very well, is not remarkably good. I doubt whether *A Tale of a Tub* be his; for he never owned it, and it is much above his usual manner.

SAMUEL JOHNSON, on Jonathan Swift

❀

Good God! what a genius I had when I wrote that book.

JONATHAN SWIFT, on himself

❀

Yes I am proud; I must be proud to see
Men, not afraid of God, afraid of me.

ALEXANDER POPE, on himself

❀

There are two ways of disliking poetry; one way is to dislike it, the other is to read Pope.

OSCAR WILDE, on Alexander Pope

❀

Dryden was a better prose-writer, and a bolder and more varied versifier than Pope. He was a more vigorous thinker, a more correct and logical declaimer, and had more of what may be called strength of mind than Pope, but he had not the same refinement and delicacy of feeling.

WILLIAM HAZLITT, on John Dryden

Ev'n copious Dryden, wanted, or forgot.
The last and greatest Art, the art to blot.

ALEXANDER POPE, on John Dryden

❀

He never heartily and sincerely praised any human being, or felt
any real enthusiasm for any subject he took up.

JOHN KEBLE, on John Dryden

❀

Mr. Johnson did not like anyone who said they were happy, or
who said anyone else was so. "It is all *cant* (he would cry), the
dog knows he is miserable all the time."

HESTER LYNCH THRALE, on Samuel Johnson

❀

Dr. Johnson's sayings would not appear so extraordinary, were
it not for his bow-wow way.

LORD PEMBROKE, on Samuel Johnson

❀

If you were to make the little fishes talk, they would talk like
whales.   OLIVER GOLDSMITH, to Samuel Johnson

Indeed, the freedom with which Dr. Johnson condemns whatever he disapproves is astonishing.

FANNY BURNEY, on Samuel Johnson

❁

You must not mind me, madam; I say strange things, but I mean no harm.   SAMUEL JOHNSON, on himself

❁

You think I love flattery, and so I do; but a little too much always disgusts me. That fellow Richardson, on the contrary, could not be contented to sail quietly down the stream of his reputation, without longing to taste the froth from every stroke of the oar.   SAMUEL JOHNSON, on Samuel Richardson

❁

Fielding had as much humour perhaps as Addison, but, having no idea of grace, is perpetually disgusting.

HORACE WALPOLE, on Henry Fielding

❁

He was dull in company, dull in his closet, dull everywhere. He was dull in a new way, and that made many people think him *great*. He was a mechanical poet.

SAMUEL JOHNSON, on Thomas Gray

Goldsmith's mind was entirely unfurnished. When he was engaged in a work, he had all his knowledge to find, which when he found, he knew how to use, but forgot it immediately after he had used it.

SIR JOSHUA REYNOLDS, on Oliver Goldsmith

❋

An inspired idiot.

HORACE WALPOLE, attributed, on Oliver Goldsmith

❋

It is amazing how little Goldsmith knows. He seldom comes where he is not more ignorant than anyone else.

SAMUEL JOHNSON, on Oliver Goldsmith

❋

Gibbon is an ugly, affected, disgusting fellow, and poisons our literary club for me. I class him among infidel wasps and venomous insects.

JAMES BOSWELL, on Edward Gibbon

❋

Edward Gibbon was a great hand for footnotes, especially if it gave him a chance to show off his Latin. He would come sniffing up to a nice, spicey morsel of scandal about the Romans and then, just as the reader expected him to dish the dirt, he'd go into his Latin routine, somewhat as follows: "in those days vice reached depths not plumbed since the reign of Caligula and it was an open secret that the notorious Empress Theodoro *in tres partes divisa erat* and that she was also addicted to the *argumentum ad hominem!*" Gibbon, prissy little fat man that he was, did that just to tease readers who flunked Caesar.

FRANK SULLIVAN, on Edward Gibbon

❀

Gibbon's style is detestable; but it is not the worst thing about him.
SAMUEL COLERIDGE, on Edward Gibbon

❀

Another damned thick, square book! Always scribble, scribble! Eh! Mr. Gibbon?

THE DUKE OF GLOUCESTER, to Edward Gibbon
upon accepting the second volume of
A History of the Decline and Fall of the Roman Empire

❀

The round-faced man in black entered, and dissipated all doubts on the subject, by beginning to talk. He did not cease while he stayed; nor has he since, that I know of.

WILLIAM HAZLITT, on Samuel Coleridge

❀

To tell the story of Coleridge without the opium is to tell the story of *Hamlet* without mentioning the ghost.

LESLIE STEPHEN, on Samuel Coleridge

I don't well know what is the reason of it, but somehow or other, though I am, when I have a mind, pretty generally beloved, yet I never could get the art of commanding respect.

ROBERT BURNS, on himself

❋

What an antithetical mind!—tenderness, roughness—delicacy, coarseness—sentiment, sensuality—soaring and grovelling, dirt and deity—all mixed up in that one compound of inspired clay!

LORD BYRON, on Robert Burns

❋

A Burns is infinitely better educated than a Byron.

THOMAS CARLYLE, on Robert Burns

❋

Then comes Sir Walter Scott with his enchantments, and by his single might checks this wave of progress, and even turns it back; sets the world in love with dreams and phantoms; with decayed and degraded systems of government; with the silliness and emptiness, sham grandeurs, sham gauds, and sham chivalries of a brainless and worthless long-vanished society. He did measureless harm; more real and lasting harm, perhaps, than any other individual that ever wrote.   MARK TWAIN, on Sir Walter Scott

I believe it was admitted by Scott
That some of his novels were rot.
How different he was from Lytton,
Who admired everything he had written!

EDMUND CLERIHEW BENTLEY,
on Sir Walter Scott and Sir Edward Bulwer-Lytton

❋

I met Sir Bulwer-Lytton. He is anxious about some scheme for some association of literary men. I detest all such associations. I hate the notion of gregarious authors. The less we have to do with each other the better.

THOMAS BABINGTON MACAULEY,
on Sir Edward Bulwer-Lytton

❋

He never wrote an invitation to dinner without an eye on posterity. BENJAMIN DISRAELI, on Sir Edward Bulwer-Lytton

❋

Bulwer Lytton I detest. He is the very pimple of the age's humbug.

NATHANIEL HAWTHORNE, on Sir Edward Bulwer-Lytton

I wish I was as cocksure of anything as Tom Macaulay is of everything.

WILLIAM LAMB, on Thomas Babington Macaulay

❁

I am at a loss to understand why people hold Miss Austen's novels at so high a rate, which seem to me vulgar in tone, sterile in artistic invention, imprisoned in their wretched conventions of English society, without genius, wit, or knowledge of the world. Never was life so pinched and narrow. The one problem in the mind of the writer is . . . marriageableness. . . . Suicide is more respectable.   RALPH WALDO EMERSON, on Jane Austen

❁

I learned the possibilities of domestic humor. I was more ambitious than she was, of course; I tried to hitch on to other things.

E. M. FORSTER, on Jane Austen

❁

Jane Austen's books, too, are absent from this library. Just that one omission alone would make a fairly good library out of a library that hadn't a book in it.

MARK TWAIN, on Jane Austen

Jane Austen

I dislike Jane, and am prejudiced, in fact, against all women writers. They are in another class. Could never see anything in *Pride and Prejudice*.

> VLADIMIR NABOKOV, on Jane Austen,
> in a letter to Edmund Wilson

❀

You are mistaken about Jane Austen. I think you ought to reread *Mansfield Park*. Her greatness is due precisely to the fact that her attitude toward her work is like that of a man, that is, of an artist, and quite unlike that of the typical woman novelist, who exploits her feminine day-dreams. . . . She is, in my opinion, one of the half dozen greatest English writers.

> EDMUND WILSON, replying
> to Vladimir Nabokov regarding Jane Austen

❀

He is the absolute monarch of words, and uses them, as Bonaparte did lives, for conquest, without more regard to their intrinsic value.   LORD BYRON, on himself

❀

He had not the intellectual equipment of a supreme modern poet; except for his genius he was an ordinary nineteenth-century English gentleman, with little culture and no ideas.

> MATTHEW ARNOLD, on Lord Byron

You speak of Lord Byron and me. There is this great difference between us. He describes what he sees, I describe what I imagine. Mine is the hardest task.

JOHN KEATS, on Lord Byron

❋

He seems to me the most vulgar-minded genius that ever produced a great effect in literature.   GEORGE ELIOT, on Lord Byron

❋

Mad, bad, and dangerous to know.

LADY CAROLINE LAMB, on Lord Byron

❋

A word to you of Lady Caroline Lamb—I speak from experience—keep clear of her —(I do not mean as a woman—that is all fair) she is a villainous intriguante—in every sense of the word—mad and malignant—capable of all and every mischief—above all—guard your connections from her society—with all her apparent absurdity there is an indefatigable and active spirit of meanness and destruction about her—which delights and often succeeds in inflicting misery.   LORD BYRON, on Lady Caroline Lamb

Lord Byron

In his youth, Wordsworth sympathized with the French Revolution, went to France, wrote good poetry, and had a natural daughter. At this period, he was a "bad" man. Then he became "good," abandoned his daughter, adopted correct principles and wrote bad poetry.

BERTRAND RUSSELL, on William Wordsworth

❀

Perhaps "alive" is scarcely the word one would apply to the "luminary" of the Lake District. Wordsworth drew his first orderly and deliberate breath in 1770, and continued the alternative processes of inhalation and exhalation until 1850.

EZRA POUND, on William Wordsworth

❀

Wordsworth is so often flat and heavy partly because his moral sense has no theatrical elements; it is an obedience, a discipline which he has not created.

WILLIAM BUTLER YEATS, on William Wordsworth

❀

Separate from the pleasure of your company, I don't much care if I never see another mountain in my life.

CHARLES LAMB, in a letter to William Wordsworth

He had no talent, but he wrote a book in which his earnestness and his sincerity, his thoughtfulness and his integrity, were so evident that, although it was quite unreadable, no one could fail to be impressed by it.

SOMERSET MAUGHAM, on Charles Lamb

❋

. . . same old sausage, fizzing and sputtering in his own grease.

HENRY JAMES, on Charles Lamb

❋

Charles Lamb I sincerely believe to be in some considerable degree insane. A more pitiful, rickety, gasping, staggering, stammering Tomfool I do not know.

THOMAS CARLYLE, on Charles Lamb

❋

Let me have my own way exactly in everything, and a sunnier and pleasanter creature does not exist.

THOMAS CARLYLE, on himself

❋

It was good of God to let Carlyle and Mrs. Carlyle marry one another and so make only two people miserable instead of four.

SAMUEL BUTLER, on Thomas Carlyle

That anyone who dressed so very badly as did Thomas Carlyle should have tried to construct a philosophy of clothes has always seemed to me one of the most pathetic things in literature.

MAX BEERBOHM, on Thomas Carlyle

❋

A style resembling either early architecture or utter dilapidation, so loose and rough it seemed; a wind-in-the-orchard style, that tumbled down here and there an appreciable fruit with uncouth bluster; sentences without commencements running to abrupt endings and smoke, like waves against a sea-wall, learned dictionary words giving a hand to street slang, and accents falling on them haphazard, like slant rays from driving clouds; all the pages in a breeze, the whole book producing a kind of electric agitation in the mind and joints.

GEORGE MEREDITH, on Thomas Carlyle

❋

Carlyle is a poet to whom nature has denied the faculty of verse.

ALFRED, LORD TENNYSON, on Thomas Carlyle

❋

In one place in *Deerslayer,* and in the restricted space of two thirds of a page, Cooper has scored 114 offenses against literary art out of a possible 115. It breaks the record.

MARK TWAIN, on James Fenimore Cooper

The craft of the woodsman, the tricks of the trapper, all the delicate art of the forest were familiar to Cooper from his youth up.

BRANDER MATTHEWS, on James Fenimore Cooper

❈

Every time a Cooper person is in peril, and absolute silence is worth four dollars a minute, he is sure to step on a dry twig. There may be a hundred handier things to step on, but that wouldn't satisfy Cooper. Cooper requires him to turn out and find a dry twig; and if he can't do it, go and borrow one. In fact, the Leatherstocking series ought to have been called the Broken Twig Series.

MARK TWAIN, on James Fenimore Cooper

❈

I have an unpurchasable mind.

PERCY BYSSHE SHELLEY, on himself

❈

The splendours, the almost supernatural beauty of the active mind of Shelley will obviously forever gild his poems and blind one to the mediocrity of thousands of his inferior lines. But the gold is an exterior gold; . . . He is almost never natural; he is almost never not intent on showing himself the champion of freedom, the Satan of a Hanoverian Heaven.

FORD MADOX FORD, on Percy Bysshe Shelley

Shelley should not be read, but inhaled through a gas pipe.

LIONEL TRILLING, on Percy Bysshe Shelley

❀

Keats is a miserable creature, hungering after sweets which he can't get; going about saying, "I am so hungry; I should so like something pleasant!"   THOMAS CARLYLE, on John Keats

❀

Such writing is a sort of mental masturbation—he is always f—gg—g his *Imagination.* I don't mean he is *indecent,* but viciously soliciting his own ideas into a state, which is neither poetry nor any thing else but a Bedlam vision produced by raw pork and opium.

LORD BYRON, on John Keats

❀

The lighthouse in a sea of absurdity.

FRIEDRICH NIETZSCHE, on Victor Hugo

❀

Ah, well! I don't know that you will ever feel that you have really met him. He is like a dim room with a little taper of personality burning on the corner of the mantel.

OLIVER WENDELL HOLMES, on Nathaniel Hawthorne

Nathaniel Hawthorne's reputation as a writer is a very pleasing fact, because his writing is not good for anything, and this is a tribute to the man.

RALPH WALDO EMERSON, on Nathaniel Hawthorne

❊

Emerson is a person who lives instinctively on ambrosia—and leaves everything indigestible on his plate.

FRIEDRICH NIETZSCHE, on Ralph Waldo Emerson

❊

Edgar Allan Poe
Was passionately fond of roe.
He always liked to chew some
When writing anything gruesome.

EDMUND CLERIHEW BENTLEY, on Edgar Allan Poe

❊

To me, Poe's prose is unreadable—like Jane Austen's. No, there is a difference. I could read his prose on a salary, but not Jane's.

MARK TWAIN, on Edgar Allan Poe and Jane Austen

❊

In junior high school I started to write imitation Edgar Allan Poe stories. I knew I had been named after a writer, my first name being Edgar. I believed my parents named me after him. Many years later I told my mother, "You realize you named me

Edgar Allan Poe

after a necrophiliac drug addict sadomasochistic latent homosexual?" She said, "Oh Edgar, stop your fooling."

E. L. DOCTOROW, on Edgar Allan Poe

❀

That Poe had a powerful intellect is undeniable: but it seems to me the intellect of a highly gifted young person before puberty. The forms which his lively curiosity takes are those in which a pre-adolescent mentality delights: wonders of nature and of mechanics and of the supernatural, cryptograms and cyphers, puzzles and labyrinths, mechanical chess-players and wild flights of speculation.

T. S. ELIOT, on Edgar Allan Poe

❀

Oh, you mean the jingleman!

RALPH WALDO EMERSON, on Edgar Allan Poe

❀

His didactics are all out of place. He has written brilliant poems, by accident; that is to say, when permitting his genius to get the better of his conversational habit of thinking, a habit deduced from German study.

EDGAR ALLAN POE, on Henry Wadsworth Longfellow

Longfellow is to poetry what the barrel-organ is to music.
  VAN WYCK BROOKS, on Henry Wadsworth Longfellow

❈

We had some tea and strawberries. . . . There was no very noteworthy conversation; the most interesting topic being that disagreeable and now wearisome one of spiritual communications, as regards which Mrs. Browning is a believer, and her husband an infidel.   NATHANIEL HAWTHORNE, on the Brownings

❈

The simple truth is that she was the poet, and I the clever person by comparison.
  ROBERT BROWNING, on Elizabeth Barrett Browning

❈

Browning used words with the violence of a horse-breaker, giving out the scent of a he-goat. But he got them to do their work.
  FORD MADOX FORD, on Robert Browning

❈

He has plenty of music in him, but he cannot get it out.
  ALFRED, LORD TENNYSON, on Robert Browning

He is very natural and simple, and rather abrupt in his manner from a constitutional shyness; a man to revolt against any effort to make him "shine." He doesn't shine—but you do not feel it difficult to believe him to be a great man whether he speaks or is silent. I assure you he smoked his pipe (a real clay pipe) after tea—with just a word of mere form to ascertain if it would throw me into fits or not.

ELIZABETH BARRETT BROWNING,
on Alfred, Lord Tennyson

❋

He could not think up to the height of his own towering style.
G. K. CHESTERTON, on Alfred, Lord Tennyson

❋

As for the author of *Uncle Tom's Cabin* her syntax was such a snare to her that it sometimes needed the combined skill of the proofreaders and the assistant editor to extricate her. Of course nothing was ever written into her work, but in changes of diction, in correction of solecisms, in transposition of phrases, the text was largely rewritten in the margin of their proofs. The soul of their art was present, but the form was so often absent, that when it was clothed on anew, it would have been hard to say whose cut the garment was of in many places.

WILLIAM DEAN HOWELLS, on Harriet Beecher Stowe

Melville has the strange, uncanny magic of sea-creatures, and some of their repulsiveness. He isn't quite a land animal. There is something slithery about him. Something always half-seas-over. In his life they said he was mad—or crazy. But he was over the border.

D. H. LAWRENCE, on Herman Melville

❀

I couldn't take Hawthorne; I still can't. I don't like anything he wrote except *The Blithedale Romance,* which is almost a novel. The others are romances. I do detest *Moby Dick* and I never finished *Pierre* or *The Ambiguities.* But then, I don't like Melville's writing. It is windy and pretentious, it is bogus Shakespeare. GORE VIDAL, on Herman Melville and Nathaniel Hawthorne

❀

Thackeray is unique. I *can* say no more, I *will* say no less.

CHARLOTTE BRONTË, on William Makepeace Thackeray

❀

I found out in the first two pages that it was a woman's writing—she *supposed* that in making a door, you last of all put in the *panels!*

THOMAS CARLYLE, after reading George Eliot's *Adam Bede*

In this vast ugliness resides a most powerful beauty which, in a very few moments steals forth and charms the mind, so that you end as I ended, in falling in love with her. Yes, behold me literally in love with this great horse-faced blue-stocking. I don't know in what the charm lies, but it is thoroughly potent. An admirable physiognomy—a delightful expression, a voice soft and rich as that of a counselling angel—a mingled sagacity and sweetness—a broad hint of a great underlying world of reserve, knowledge, pride and power—a great feminine dignity and character in these massively plain features—a hundred conflicting shades of consciousness and simpleness—shyness and frankness—graciousness and remote indifference—these are some of the more definite elements of her personality. . . . Altogether, she has a larger circumference than any woman I have ever seen.

HENRY JAMES, on George Eliot

❁

I believe she would have given all her genius and all her fame to be beautiful. Perhaps few women ever existed more anxious to be pretty than she, and more angrily conscious of the circumstance that she was *not* pretty.

GEORGE SMITH, on Charlotte Brontë

❁

I wish critics would judge me as an author, not as a woman.

CHARLOTTE BRONTË, on herself, to George Henry Lewes

He is not as handsome as his photographs—or his poetry.

HENRY JAMES, on Matthew Arnold

❀

You may rely on it that you have the best of me in my books, and that I am not worth seeing personally.

HENRY DAVID THOREAU, on himself

❀

He is as ugly as sin, long-nosed, queer-mouthed, and with uncouth and somewhat rustic, although courteous manners, corresponding very well with such an exterior. But his ugliness is of an honest and agreeable fashion, and becomes him much better than beauty.

NATHANIEL HAWTHORNE, on Henry David Thoreau

❀

Thoreau is unique among writers in that those who admire him find him uncomfortable to live with—a regular hairshirt of a man.

E. B. WHITE, on Henry David Thoreau

❀

Whatever question there may be of his talent, there can none I think be of his genius. It was a slim and crooked one, but it was eminently personal.

HENRY JAMES, on Henry David Thoreau

He was a man of great talent—I do not deny it: and skill, yes, skill—I do not deny that. But inspiration? I doubt it.

WALT WHITMAN, on James Russell Lowell

❋

All children ought to love him. I know two that do, and read his books ten times for once that they peruse the dismal preachments of their father. I know one when she is unhappy reads *Nicholas Nickleby;* when she is tired reads *Nicholas Nickleby;* when she is in bed reads *Nicholas Nickleby;* when she has nothing to do reads *Nicholas Nickleby,* and when she has finished the book reads *Nicholas Nickleby* over again. This candid young critic, at ten years of age, said, "I like Mr. Dickens's books much better than your books, Papa"; and frequently expressed her desire that the latter author should write a book like one of Mr. Dickens's books. Who can?

WILLIAM MAKEPEACE THACKERAY, on Charles Dickens

❋

One must have a heart of stone to read the death of Little Nell by Dickens without laughing.

OSCAR WILDE, on Charles Dickens

Of Dickens's style it is impossible to speak in praise. It is jerky, ungrammatical, and created by himself in defiance of rules—almost as completely as that created by Carlyle. To readers who have taught themselves to regard language, it must therefore be unpleasant. . . . No young novelist should ever dare to imitate the style of Dickens. If such a one wants a model for his language, let him take Thackeray.

ANTHONY TROLLOPE, on Charles Dickens,
William Makepeace Thackeray, and Thomas Carlyle

❊

Trollope! Did anybody bear a name that predicted a style more Trollopy?   GEORGE MOORE, on Anthony Trollope

❊

I saw the book, but I didn't read it at all—didn't think it worth reading. Mother thought as I did.

GEORGE WHITMAN, brother of Walt, on *Leaves of Grass*

❊

He is neither afraid of being slangy nor of being dull; nor, let me add, of being ridiculous. The result is the most surprising compound of plain grandeur, sentimental affection, and downright nonsense.

ROBERT LOUIS STEVENSON, on Walt Whitman

Do I contradict myself?
Very well then I contradict myself,
(I am large, I contain multitudes).

WALT WHITMAN, on himself

❋

This awful Whitman. This post-mortem poet. This poet with
the private soul leaking out of him all the time. All his privacy
leaking out in a sort of dribble, oozing into the universe.

D. H. LAWRENCE, on Walt Whitman

❋

He is America. His crudity is an exceeding great stench but it is
America. He is a hollow place in the rock that echoes with his
time. He does "chant the crucial stage" and he is the "voice tri-
umphant." He is disgusting. He is an exceedingly nauseating
pill, but he accomplishes his mission.

EZRA POUND, on Walt Whitman

❋

At his best, a sort of daintily dressed Walt Whitman.

G. K. CHESTERTON, on George Meredith

❋

Meredith is, to me, chiefly a stink. I should never write on him
as I detest him too much ever to trust myself as a critic of him.

EZRA POUND, on George Meredith

Ah! Meredith! Who can define him? His style is chaos illumined by flashes of lightning. As a writer he has mastered everything except language: as a novelist he can do everything except tell a story: as an artist he is everything except articulate.

OSCAR WILDE, on George Meredith

❋

I suppose my model is nearly always Dostoevsky, a man of very strong convictions, but his characters illustrated and incarnated in the most powerful themes and issues and trends of his day. I think maybe the greatest novel of all times is the *Brothers Karamazov.*   WALKER PERCY, on Fyodor Dostoevsky

❋

My God, think of how morbid and depressing Dostoevsky would have been if he could have gotten hold of some of the juicy work of Dr. Wilhelm Stekel, say *Sadism and Masochism.*

WILLIAM STYRON, on Fyodor Dostoevsky

❋

I'm a heretic about Tolstoy. I really don't see *War and Peace* as a great novel because it seems constantly to be trying to prove that nobody who was in the war knew what was going on. . . . The point's very much better done, I think, by Joseph de Maistre.   REBECCA WEST, on Leo Tolstoy

Fyodor Dostoevsky

I started out very quiet and I beat Mr. Turgenev. Then I trained hard and I beat Mr. de Maupassant. I've fought two draws with Mr. Stendhal, and I think I had an edge in the last one. But nobody's going to get me in any ring with Mr. Tolstoy unless I'm crazy or I keep getting better.

ERNEST HEMINGWAY, on himself and Leo Tolstoy

❋

Christina Rossetti is too little known, except by some of her moralistic verses; she had a most delicate command of rhythm, . . . a delicate sense of the sound of words, and a highly competent technical ability which never appeared laboured because of its simplicity. . . . But it is her perspective of life that interests me most: sweet, small and narrow, delicate to the point of elusion.

DYLAN THOMAS, on Christina Rossetti

❋

Christine [sic] has the great distinction of being a born poet, as she seems to have known very well herself. But if I were bringing a case against God she is one of the first witnesses I should call. It is melancholy reading. First she starved herself of love, which meant also of life; then of poetry in deference to what she thought her religion demanded. . . . Consequently, as I think, she starved into austere emaciation a very fine original gift.

VIRGINIA WOOLF, on Christina Rossetti

His sister Emily is called in Amherst "the myth." She has not been out of her house for fifteen years. One inevitably thinks of Miss Havisham in speaking of her. She writes the strangest poems, and very remarkable ones. She is in many respects a genius. She wears always white, and has her hair arranged as was the fashion fifteen years ago when she went into retirement. She wanted me to come and sing to her, but she would not see me. She has frequently sent me flowers and poems and we have a very pleasant friendship in that way.

MABEL LOOMIS TODD, on Emily Dickinson

❋

And ultimately one simply sighs at Miss Dickinson's singular perversity, her lapses and tyrannies, and accepts them as an inevitable part of the strange and original genius that she was. The lapses and tyrannies become a positive charm—one even suspects they were deliberate.

CONRAD AIKEN, on Emily Dickinson

❋

How wrong Emily Dickinson was! Hope is not "the thing with feathers." The thing with feathers has turned out to be my nephew. I must take him to a specialist in Zurich.

WOODY ALLEN, on Emily Dickinson

Emily Dickinson

Miss Alcott's experience of human nature has been small, as we should suppose her admiration of it is nevertheless great.

HENRY JAMES, on Louisa May Alcott

❀

Mark Twain and I are in very much the same position. We have to put things in such a way as to make people, who would otherwise hang us, believe that we are joking.

GEORGE BERNARD SHAW, on Mark Twain

❀

If Mr. Clemens cannot think of something better to tell our pure-minded lads and lasses, he had best stop writing for them.

LOUISA MAY ALCOTT, on *Huckleberry Finn* by Mark Twain (Samuel Clemens)

❀

He had one of the more wicked minds ever going.

TRUMAN CAPOTE, on Mark Twain

❀

I prefer dead writers because you don't run into them at parties. Twain I *really* love. I know he's very highly regarded, but I don't think he's taken very seriously. He wrote humorous things and humorous writers are never taken seriously enough.

FRAN LEBOWITZ, on Mark Twain

A hack writer who would not have been considered fourth rate in Europe, who tricked out a few of the old proven "sure fire" literary skeletons with sufficient local color to intrigue the superficial and the lazy.   WILLIAM FAULKNER, on Mark Twain

❂

My books are water; those of the great geniuses are wine. Everybody drinks water.   MARK TWAIN, on himself

❂

He was showy, meretricious, insincere; and he constantly advertised these qualities in his dress. He was distinctly pretty, in spite of the fact that his face was badly pitted with smallpox. In the days when he could afford it—and in the days when he couldn't— his clothes always exceeded the fashion by a shade or two.

MARK TWAIN, on Bret Harte

❂

Bret Harte illuminated everything he touched. Now in shilling-shockers contracted for, years in advance at so many points a hundred words, he slaughters cowboys to make cockneys sit up or hashes up a short story to serve as jam between commercial sandwiches in sloppy popular magazines.

AMBROSE BIERCE, on Bret Harte

Mark Twain

In the early days I liked Bret Harte, and so did the others; but by and by I got over it; so did the others.

MARK TWAIN, on Bret Harte

❋

I have not a penny worth of poetry in me. I treat everything with indifference and spend two thirds of my time being utterly bored with myself. I spend the other third of it writing material that I sell at as high a price as possible, regretting having to do this wretched type of work that has brought me the distinction of being known and famous for you!

GUY DE MAUPASSANT, on himself, in a letter to Marie Bashkirtseff

❋

Nothing is my last word about anything—I am interminably supersubtle and analytic—and with the blessing of heaven, I shall live to make all sorts of representations of all sorts of things. It will take a lot cleverer person than myself to discover my last impression—amongst all these things—of anything.

HENRY JAMES, on himself

❋

Henry James has a mind so fine no idea could violate it.

T. S. ELIOT, on Henry James

Henry James would have been vastly improved as a novelist by a few whiffs from the Chicago stockyards.

H. L. MENCKEN, on Henry James

❋

That's the trouble with James. You get bored with him finally. He lived in a time of four-wheelers, and no bombs, and the problems then seemed a bit special and separate. That's one reason you feel restless reading him.

JAMES THURBER, on Henry James

❋

He spares no resource in telling of his dead inventions. . . . Bare verbs he rarely tolerates. He splits infinitives and fills them up with adverbial stuffing. He presses the passing colloquialism into his service. His vast paragraphs sweat and struggle; they could not sweat and elbow and struggle more if God Himself was the processional meaning to which they sought to come.

H. G. WELLS, on Henry James

❋

I don't think he thought the world had any moral purpose. I think he disbelieved in God.

JORGE LUIS BORGES, on Henry James

I have just read a long novel by Henry James. Much of it made me think of the priest condemned for a long space to confess nuns.

WILLIAM BUTLER YEATS, on Henry James

❊

Mr. Henry James writes fiction as if it were a painful duty.

OSCAR WILDE, on Henry James

❊

I once dreamed I was in Iowa City at a party in my house. Henry James was there, and he was sitting in a corner, pouring whisky into his high silk hat. Two weeks later I came to New York, and on Seventh Avenue I found a book, *Memories, by a Publisher's Wife*, in which I read, "Henry James was here the other evening, and was so drunk that he sat in a corner, pouring whiskey into his high silk hat"—It was a very obscure little memoir, and I had never read it or heard of it, or known that Henry in actuality would take a drink.

MARGUERITE YOUNG, on Henry James

❊

When he isn't being a great and magnificent author, he certainly can be a very fussy and tiresome one.

EZRA POUND, on Henry James

The nicest old lady I ever met.   **4**
> WILLIAM FAULKNER, on Henry James

❁

I have always said that you were far away the superior to your brother Henry, and that you could have cut him quite out, if you had turned your pen that way.
> HENRY ADAMS, to William James

❁

There was, in spite of his playfullness, a deep sadness about James. You felt that he had just stepped out of this sadness in order to meet you, and was to go back into it the moment you left him.   JOHN JAY CHAPMAN, on William James

❁

When I happened to fall in with him on the street, he could be delightful, but when I called at his house and he was posing to himself as the old cardinal he could turn everything to dust and ashes. After a tiresome day's work one didn't care to have one's powers of resistance taxed by discourse of that sort, so I called rarely.   OLIVER WENDELL HOLMES, on Henry Adams

❁

Hardy went down to botanize in the swamps . . . he became a sort of village atheist brooding and blaspheming over the village idiot.   G. K. CHESTERTON, on Thomas Hardy

He seems to me to have written as nearly for the sake of "self-expression" as a man well can; and the self which he had to express does not strike me as a particularly wholesome or edifying matter of communication. He was indifferent even to the prescripts of good writing: he wrote sometimes overpoweringly well, but always very carelessly; at times his style touches sublimity without ever having passed through the stage of being good.

T. S. ELIOT, on Thomas Hardy

❋

The gloom is not even relieved by a little elegance of diction.

LYTTON STRACHEY, on the poems of Thomas Hardy

❋

Some of Bierce's bitterness may have been caused by an unfortunate accident during the Civil War. In the *Battle for Kennesaw Mountain,* he received a musket ball through his head. Though the two holes eventually healed up, Bierce still felt hurt.

RICHARD ARMOUR, on Ambrose Bierce

❋

Bierce would bury his best friend with a sigh of relief, and express satisfaction that he was done with him.

JACK LONDON, on Ambrose Bierce

His pathos is bathos, his sentiment sediment, his "homely philosophy" brute platitudes—beasts of the field of thought.

AMBROSE BIERCE, on James Riley

❀

He was not interested, as Eugene Field was, in expanding or exploring a child's imagination; he looked only for a situation that would bring tears to a reader's eyes. The poem was never written for the child; it was written to commercialize the child's feelings.   CARLIN T. KINDILIEN, on James Riley

❀

I am a rogue at egotism myself; and, to be plain, I have rarely or never liked a man who was not.

ROBERT LOUIS STEVENSON, on himself

❀

There is always in his work a certain clean-cut angularity which makes us remember that he was fond of cutting wood with an axe.

G. K. CHESTERTON, on Robert Louis Stevenson

❀

Stevenson's letters most disappointing also. I see that romantic surroundings are the worst surroundings possible for a romantic writer.   In *Gower Street,* Stevenson could have written a new *Trois Mousquetaires.* In Samoa he wrote letters to the *Times* about Germans. I see also the traces of a terrible strain to lead a

Robert Louis Stevenson

natural life. To chop wood with any advantage to oneself or profit to others, one should not be able to describe the process. In point of fact the natural life is the unconscious life. Stevenson merely extended the sphere of the artificial by taking to digging.

OSCAR WILDE, on Robert Louis Stevenson

❀

He writes like a Pakistani who has learned English when he was twelve years old in order to become a chartered accountant.

JOHN OSBORNE, on George Bernard Shaw

❀

I remember coming across him at the Grand Canyon and finding him peevish, refusing to admire it or even look at it properly. He was jealous.

J. B. PRIESTLEY, on George Bernard Shaw

❀

An excellent man: he has no enemies; and none of his friends like him.   OSCAR WILDE, on George Bernard Shaw

❀

Mr. Shaw is (I suspect) the only man on earth who has never written any poetry.

G. K. CHESTERTON, on George Bernard Shaw

Shaw is almost a hopeless subject because there is nothing interesting to be said about him that he has not already said about himself.   FRANK HARRIS, on George Bernard Shaw

❀

He will fill his fountain pen with your heart's blood, and sell your most sacred emotions on the stage. He is a mass of imagination with no heart. He is a writing and talking machine that has worked for nearly forty years until its skill is devilish. . . . All his goods are in the shop window, and he'll steal your goods and put them there too.   GEORGE BERNARD SHAW, on himself

❀

George Too Shaw To Be Good.
          DYLAN THOMAS, on George Bernard Shaw

❀

Shaw, one day you will eat a pork chop and then god help all women.
     MRS. PAT CAMPBELL, attributed, on George Bernard Shaw

❀

Shaw's relations with women have always been gallant, coy even. The number he has surrendered to physically have been few—perhaps not half a dozen in all—the first man to have cut a swathe through the theatre and left it strewn with virgins.
          FRANK HARRIS, on George Bernard Shaw

He is invited to all the great houses of England—once.

OSCAR WILDE, on Frank Harris

❀

Harris really thought he was wonderful. Once he told me he was going to live to be a hundred. When I asked him what the formula was, he told me it was very simple. He said: "I've bought myself a stomach pump and one half hour after dinner I pump myself out." Can you imagine that? Well, it didn't work. It's a wonder it didn't kill him sooner.

JAMES THURBER, on Frank Harris

❀

What has Oscar in common with art, except that he dines at our tables and picks from our platters the plums for the pudding that he peddles in the provinces? Oscar—the amiable, irresponsible, esurient Oscar—with no more sense of a picture than he has of the fit of a coat—has the courage of the opinions . . . of others!

JAMES MCNEIL WHISTLER, on Oscar Wilde

❀

Oscar Wilde's talent seems to me essentially rootless, something growing in a glass in a little water.

GEORGE MOORE, on Oscar Wilde

His manner had hardened to meet opposition and at times he allowed one to see an unpardonable insolence. His charm was acquired and systematised, a mask which he wore only when it pleased him.   WILLIAM BUTLER YEATS, on Oscar Wilde

❀

It is curious how vanity helps the successful man and wrecks the failure. In old days half of my strength was my vanity.

OSCAR WILDE, on himself

❀

He loves first editions, especially of women.

OSCAR WILDE, on Leonard Smithers

❀

"Do you know George Moore?" I asked him [Oscar Wilde] one day when he had been rolling the British Zola's novels round the ring. "Know him? I know him so well that I haven't spoken to him in ten years."

VINCENT O'SULLIVAN, on George Moore

❀

Susan Mitchell sensed something lacking. Women are like that. She wrote, "Some men kiss and do not tell, some kiss and tell; but George Moore told and did not kiss."

OLIVER ST. JOHN GOGARTY, on George Moore

Oscar Wilde

The technical perfection of the novels of Mr. George Moore does not prevent them from being faultlessly dead.

Q. D. LEAVIS, on George Moore

❊

He leads his readers to the latrine and locks them in.

OSCAR WILDE, on George Moore

❊

At present Conrad is out of fashion, ostensibly because of his florid style and redundant adjectives (for my part I like a florid style: if your motto is "Cut out the adjectives", why not go a bit further and revert to a system of grunts and squeals, like the animals?), but actually, I suspect, because he was a gentleman, a type hated by modern intelligentsia. He is pretty certain to come back in favour. One of the surest signs of his genius is that women dislike his books.

GEORGE ORWELL, on Joseph Conrad

❊

Conrad spent the day finding the *mot juste,* and then killed it.

FORD MADOX FORD, on Joseph Conrad

It is agreed by most of the people I know that Conrad is a bad writer, just as it is agreed that T. S. Eliot is a good writer. If I knew that by grinding Mr. Eliot into a fine dry powder and sprinkling that powder on Mr. Conrad's grave, Mr. Conrad would shortly appear, looking very annoyed at the forced return and commence writing, I would leave for London early tomorrow morning with a sausage grinder.

ERNEST HEMINGWAY, on Joseph Conrad and T. S. Eliot

❀

I learned all I know of Literature from Conrad—and England has learned all it knows of Literature from me.

FORD MADOX FORD, on himself and Joseph Conrad

❀

His mind was like a Roquefort cheese, so ripe that it was palpably falling to pieces.

VAN WYCK BROOKS, on Ford Madox Ford

❀

I once told Fordie that if he were placed naked and alone in a room without furniture, I would come back in an hour and find total confusion. EZRA POUND, on Ford Madox Ford

❀

Freud Madox Fraud.

SIR OSBERT SITWELL, on Ford Madox Ford

The connecting link is Wells's belief in Science. He is saying all the time, if only the small shopkeeper could acquire a scientific outlook, his troubles would be ended. And of course he believes that this is going to happen, probably in the quite near future. A few more million pounds for scientific research, a few more generations scientifically educated, a few more superstitions shovelled into the dustbin, and the job is done.

GEORGE ORWELL, on H. G. Wells

❋

I stopped thinking about him when he became a thinker.

LYTTON STRACHEY, on H. G. Wells

❋

I had a very unhappy time with H. G. Wells, because I was a victim of a sort of sadist situation. Partly people disapproved of H. G. so much less than they did of me, and they were very horrible to me, and it was very hard. It was particularly hard later, people being horrid to me because I was living with H. G., when I was trying as hard as I could to leave him. It was really absurd, and now I think it's rather funny, but it wasn't funny at the time.

REBECCA WEST, on herself and H. G. Wells

My stay at Stone Cottage [Yeats's home] will not be in the least profitable. I detest the country. Yeats will amuse me part of the time and bore me to death with psychical research the rest. I regard the visit as a duty to posterity.

EZRA POUND, on William Butler Yeats

❋

I am sorry that I have not led a more exciting existence, so that I might offer a more interesting biographical sketch; but I am one of those fellows who has few adventures and always gets to the fire after it is out.   EDGAR RICE BURROUGHS, on himself

❋

Tell him that some men are more interesting than their books but my book is more interesting than its man. Tell him that Frank Harris found me rude and Wilfrid Blunt found me dull. Tell him anything less that you think will put him off.

A. E. HOUSMAN, in a letter to his publisher,
Grant Richards, regarding an interview request

❋

Housman is dry, soft, shy, prickly, smooth, conventional, silent, feminine, fussy, persnickety, sensitive, tidy, greedy, and a touch of a toper. . . . A *bon bourgeois* who has seen more sensitive days. He does not talk much except about food. And at 10:30 he rises to take his leave.

SIR HAROLD NICOLSON, on A. E. Housman

Housman is one of my heroes and always has been. He was a
detestable and miserable man. Arrogant, unspeakably lonely,
cruel, and so on, but an absolutely marvelous minor poet, I
think, and a great scholar. And I'm about *equally* interested in
those two activities. In him they are perfectly distinct. You are
dealing with an absolute schizophrenic.

JOHN BERRYMAN, on A. E. Housman

❋

The first highly cultivated and brilliant woman I had ever
known. I stood a little in awe of her, as I always did in the pres-
ence of intellectual superiority, and liked best to sit silent and listen to a conversation which I still think almost the best of its day.

EDITH WHARTON, on Violet Piaget
(who used the pen name Vernon Lee)

❋

Mrs. Wharton, do you know what's the matter with you?
You don't know anything about life.

F. SCOTT FITZGERALD, to Edith Wharton

❋

She was always ready with a cold stare for those who encroached
in any way on the small caste-prerogatives that she valued so much.

VAN WYCK BROOKS, on Edith Wharton

The fact is that neither Mr. Galsworthy nor Mr. Kipling has a spark of the woman in him. Thus all their qualities seem to a woman, if one may generalise, crude and immature. They lack suggestive power. And when a book lacks suggestive power, however hard it hits the surface of the mind it cannot penetrate within.

VIRGINIA WOOLF, on John Galsworthy
and Rudyard Kipling

❀

The thing that strikes one about Galsworthy is that though he's trying to be iconoclastic, he has been utterly unable to move his mind outside the wealthy bourgeois society he is attacking. . . . All he conceives to be wrong is that human beings are a little too inhumane, a little too fond of money, and aesthetically not quite sensitive enough. When he sets out to depict what he conceives as the desirable type of human being, it turns out to be simply a cultivated, humanitarian version of the upper-middle-class rentier, the sort of person who in those days used to haunt picture galleries in Italy and subscribe heavily to the Society for the Prevention of Cruelty to Animals.

GEORGE ORWELL, on John Galsworthy

❀

I enjoy meeting authors tremendously, but more on my own level. I got the impression that Arnold Bennett was awfully pretentious. I don't know why, I suppose it was just his manner.

They all seemed to be priding themselves on being terribly great authors.   P. G. WODEHOUSE, on Arnold Bennett

❋

I remember that once, beating his knee with his clenched fist to force the words through his writhing lips, he said, "I am a nice man." He was.

SOMERSET MAUGHAM, on Arnold Bennett

❋

He was thin to emaciation, his face was gaunt and unshaven, a thin dark moustache straggled on his upper lip, his black hair grew low on his forehead and was shaggy and unkempt. His grey clothes were much the worse for wear and fitted him so badly it seemed unlikely he had ever been measured for them.

WILLA CATHER, on Stephen Crane

❋

Tolstoy made the writing of Stephen Crane on the Civil War seem like the brilliant imagining of a sick boy who had never seen war but had only read the battle chronicles and seen the Brady photographs that I had read and seen at my grandparents' house.

ERNEST HEMINGWAY, on Stephen Crane

I learned ways of looking at character from him. The modern subconscious way. He gave me as much of the modern way as I could take. I couldn't read Freud or Jung myself; it had to be filtered to me.   E. M. FORSTER, on Marcel Proust

❀

You have to be over thirty to enjoy Proust.
                    GORE VIDAL, on Marcel Proust

❀

If I had any model at all it was Flaubert. The only thing I have in common with Proust is that if Proust was American and living in New York City in 1980, he would write about the same things that I do. Other than that, we have nothing in common.
                    TRUMAN CAPOTE, on Gustav Flaubert,
                    Marcel Proust, and himself

❀

His skittish over ingenious mind makes one shy (like a horse). Not straightforward, but has a good engine in his head.
                    VIRGINIA WOOLF, on G. K. Chesterton

❀

Apart from vanity or mock modesty (which healthy people always use as jokes) my real judgement of my own work is that I have spoilt a number of jolly good ideas in my time.
                    G. K. CHESTERTON, on himself

Marcel Proust

Chesterton is like a vile scum on a pond. . . . All his slop . . .

EZRA POUND, on G. K. Chesterton

❊

We got along on just sort of "how do you do" terms. I remember walking back from a cricket match at Lords in London, and Maugham came along on the other side. He looked at me and I looked at him, and we were thinking the same thing: Oh my God, shall we have to stop and talk? Fortunately, we didn't.

P. G. WODEHOUSE, on Somerset Maugham

❊

He couldn't write for toffee, bless his heart. He wrote conventional short stories, much inferior to the work of other people. But they were much better than his plays, which were too frightful. He was an extremely intelligent man, though, not a bit clever or cold or cynical. I know of many affectionate things he did. He had a great capacity for falling in love with the wrong people. His taste seemed to give way under him so extraordinarily sometimes. He fascinated me by his appearance; he was so neatly made, like a swordstick that fits just so.

REBECCA WEST, on Somerset Maugham

❊

Very little gold had come the way of Sir Max. Although few writers have acquired his réclame—he has since his first success had a legendary quality—yet his books were sold in very small quantities and today are out of print. It is rather terrible to know that the successful Somerset Maugham criticized Max as being someone whose shirt-cuffs were generally dirty.

CECIL BEATON, on Max Beerbohm

❋

It always makes me cross when Max is called "The Incomparable Max." He is not incomparable at all, and in fact compares very poorly with Harold Nicolson, as a stylist, a wit, and an observer of human nature. He is a shallow, affected, self-conscious fribble—so there.

VITA SACKVILLE-WEST, on Max Beerbohm

❋

We went to tea with Max Beerbohm who is in a little house near Stroud. A delicious little old dandy, very quick in mind still. A touch of Ronnie Knox and of Harold Acton. "The tongue has, correct me if I am wrong, seven follicles in adult life." Much of what he said would have been commonplace but for his exquisite delivery.

EVELYN WAUGH, on Max Beerbohm

❋

He has the most remarkable and seductive genius—and I should say about the smallest in the world.

LYTTON STRACHEY, on Max Beerbohm

When first I met him, in Baltimore, he received me so nicely. He was charming. And later . . . so sympathetic, so kind. And then—you know—his books kept coming out and occasionally I was asked to review them. I couldn't, you know, abide them. He was a genius, a very great genius, and I felt that he was debasing his genius by what he wrote. And I couldn't refrain from saying so. It went on and on. Friends of his and mine kept saying that he was so pained and shocked by what I wrote, but I couldn't stop. As his publication increased, so did my derogation. He didn't stop, I *couldn't* stop. I meant to, I wanted to, but I couldn't.   MAX BEERBOHM, on Rudyard Kipling

❊

Mr. Kipling is a laureate without laurels. He is a neglected celebrity. The arrival of a new book of his verse is not likely to stir the slightest ripple on the surface of our conversational intelligentsia.   T. S. ELIOT, on Rudyard Kipling

❊

He is a man of the world, with all the narrowness that belongs to those imprisoned on that planet.

G. K. CHESTERTON, on Rudyard Kipling

I spent the better part of forty years trying to induce him to reform and electrify his manner of writing, but so far as I am aware with no more effect than if I had sought to [get him to] take up golf or abandon his belief in non-Euclidian arcana.

H. L. MENCKEN, on Theodore Dreiser

❀

To sit up and criticize me for saying "vest" instead of "waistcoat," to talk about my splitting the infinitive and using vulgar commonplaces here and there, when the tragedy of a man's life is being displayed, is silly. More, it is ridiculous. It makes me feel that American Criticism is the joke that English authorities maintain it to be. THEODORE DREISER, on himself

❀

Theodore Dreiser
Should ought to write nicer.

DOROTHY PARKER, on Theodore Dreiser

❀

How much nicer, finer, bigger you are intrinsically, than your poetry is. D. H. LAWRENCE, on Amy Lowell

❀

Our only hippo-poetess. EZRA POUND, on Amy Lowell

Her style is so deftly a part of her theme that to the uncomprehending, to the seeker after verbal glass jewels, she is not perceivable as a "stylist" at all.

SINCLAIR LEWIS, on Willa Cather

❁

When Willa talked of what she hated, her whole personality changed. Her chin hardened, her shoulders changed. Her chin hardened, her shoulders pushed forward, and one felt that the rigors of her life had made her tough or touchy. Her emotional nature was disciplined on the surface; but not far below burned a fiery surface.

ELIZABETH SHEPLEY SERGEANT, on Willa Cather

❁

Forster gave my notion of personality a sufficient shock that I could not manage to write in the third person. Forster, after all, had a developed view of the world; I did not.

NORMAN MAILER, on E. M. Forster

❁

E. M. Forster never gets any further than warming the teapot. He's a rare fine hand at that. Feel this teapot. Is it not beautifully warm? Yes, but there ain't going to be no tea.

KATHERINE MANSFIELD, on E. M. Forster

As a matter of fact Anderson is a man of practically no ideas—but he is one of the very best and finest writers in the English language today. God, can he write.

F. SCOTT FITZGERALD, on Sherwood Anderson

❋

I think Frost is a finer poet than Eliot. I mean, a finer *poet*. But I suppose Eliot was a far more intelligent man; however, intelligence has little to do with poetry. Poetry springs from something deeper; it's beyond intelligence. It may not even be linked with wisdom. It's a thing of its own; it has a nature of its own. Undefinable.

JORGE LUIS BORGES, on Robert Frost and T. S. Eliot

❋

I don't care much for Frost, and have never been able to understand his reputation. He says a good thing now and then, but with a strange way of averting his eyes while saying it which may be profound and may be poppycock. If it were thought that anything I wrote was influenced by Robert Frost, I would take that particular work of mine, shred it, and flush it down the toilet, hoping not to clog the pipes.

JAMES DICKEY, on Robert Frost

Here is the difference between Dante, Milton, and me. They wrote about hell and never saw the place. I wrote about Chicago after looking the town over for years and years.

CARL SANDBURG, on Dante, John Milton, and himself

❈

There are moments when one is tempted to feel that the cruelest thing that has happened to Lincoln since he was shot by Booth has been to fall into the hands of Carl Sandburg.

EDMUND WILSON, on Carl Sandburg winning the Pulitzer Prize for *Abraham Lincoln*

❈

I'm furious at the critical attitude toward Carl Sandburg! It's largely the work of Bunny Wilson, who was far from being the critic he's supposed to be. He was a very small-minded, petty, jealous, mean man and a stinker of the first order, and I'm saying those words for all eternity, I mean them. He hated Carl. He wrote a review of Carl's enormous *Lincoln* which was contemptuous, demeaning, belittling, and, as for Carl's being a poet, he disposed of that in a couple of well-chosen sentences.

ARCHIBALD MACLEISH, on Edmund Wilson's criticism of Carl Sandburg

❈

I have been the creative literary mind of the century.

GERTRUDE STEIN, on herself

She and G.B.S. were the two great literary egotists of their
time. G.B.S. made good his claims and Miss Stein reiterated
hers, reiteration being her specialty.

CLIFTON FADIMAN, on George Bernard Shaw
and Gertrude Stein

❀

It's a shame you never knew her before she went to pot. You
know a funny thing, she never could write dialogue. It was terrible. She learned to do it from my stuff. . . . She never could
forgive learning that and she was afraid people would notice it,
where she'd learned it, so she had to attack me. It's a funny
racket, really. But I swear she was damned nice before she got
ambitious. ERNEST HEMINGWAY, on Gertrude Stein

❀

What an old covered-wagon she is!

F. SCOTT FITZGERALD, on Gertrude Stein

❀

Gertrude Stein arrived in America and said that there were two
people that she wanted to meet. They were both in California at
that minute—Chaplin and Dash. And we were invited to dinner
at the house of a friend of Miss Stein; Charlie Chaplin, Dash,
and myself, Paulette Goddard, Miss Toklas, our host and host-
ess, and another man. There was this magnificent china and lace
tablecloth. Chaplin turned over his coffee cup, nowhere near

Stein, just all over this beautiful cloth, and the first thing Miss Stein said was, "Don't worry, it didn't get on me." She was miles away from him. She said it perfectly seriously. Then she told Dash he was the only American writer who wrote well about women. He was very pleased.

LILLIAN HELLMAN, on Gertrude Stein,
Charlie Chaplin, and Dashiell Hammett

❋

Of all the honours that fell upon Virginia's head, none, I think, pleased her more than the *Evening Standard* Award for the Tallest Woman Writer of 1927, an award she took by a neck from Elizabeth Bowen. And rightly, I think, for she was in a very real sense the tallest writer I have ever known. Which is not to say that her stories were tall. They were not. They were short. But she did stand head and shoulders above her contemporaries, and sometimes of course, much more so.

ARNOLD BENNETT, on Virginia Woolf

❋

She was one of the most beautiful women I've met in my life, really absolutely stunning, in a very strange way. Of course, she was middle-aged when I knew her. She had the quality that manic-depressive people have of being up to the sky one minute, down into despair and darkness the next. She had these terrible phases, as we know now; but what one saw was her tremendous animation and fun, on a gossipy level. She loved tea table talk.

One time I was at her place with a lot of people, and something happened to me that's never again happened in my life. We had tea, and she said, "Do stay for dinner." So I did and sat there absolutely enthralled. And suddenly, with a terrible shock, at about ten in the evening, I remembered that I was supposed to be going on a very romantic trip to Paris with someone who was in fact waiting at the airport at that moment. I had completely forgotten about it. She had that effect on people.

CHRISTOPHER ISHERWOOD, on Virginia Woolf

❀

I get courage by reading Virginia Woolf's *Writer's Diary;* I feel very akin to her, although my book reads like a slick best-seller. Her moods and neuroses are amazing. You must read this diary.

SYLVIA PLATH, in a letter to her mother

❀

Virginia Woolf's writing is no more than glamorous knitting. I believe she must have a pattern somewhere.

EDITH SITWELL, on Virginia Woolf

❀

She had been a peculiar kind of snob without really belonging to a social group with whom to be snobbish.

EDMUND WILSON, on Virginia Woolf

Virginia Woolf

An extraordinarily handsome man! He gave the impression of being a great surgeon, but not a writer at all. And he was a surgeon, he was not a writer. He used to wear white surgeon's coats all the time and that increased the impression and he had this queer, ax-like face with this enormous jaw, the biggest jaw I have ever seen on a human being. I once did a talk on Joyce in which I mentioned that he had the biggest chin I had ever seen on a human being and T. S. Eliot wrote a letter saying that he had often seen chins as big as that on other Irishmen. Well, I didn't know how to reply to that.

FRANK O'CONNOR, on James Joyce

❁

I could not write the words Mr. Joyce uses: my prudish hands would refuse to form the letters.

GEORGE BERNARD SHAW, on James Joyce

❁

I get terribly depressed when the place is always the same, the narrator's always the same, and the stories are similar. One of the saddest books I've ever read was *Dubliners,* which is all about Dublin, about depressives who are trapped, who can't escape, who can't get away, and at the end of *Dubliners* you want to cry for those people.

PAUL THEROUX, on James Joyce

I admire Joyce immensely, of course; I've written a good deal about him. But he has the true Jesuitical mind—as he himself noted—plotting, calculating, outlining, dissecting: In *Portrait of the Artist as a Young Man,* Stephen experiences the "seven deadly sins" in a programmatic way, for instance; once one knows the key, the story seems willed, artificial, slightly tainted by the author's intention. It's ideal fiction for teaching, however.

JOYCE CAROL OATES, on James Joyce

❋

James Joyce has not influenced me in any manner whatsoever.

VLADIMIR NABOKOV, on James Joyce

❋

Do not forget that my first great book, *Three Lives*, was published in 1908. That was long before *Ulysses*. But Joyce *has* done *something.* His influence, however, is local.

GERTRUDE STEIN, on James Joyce

❋

The key to reading *Ulysses* is to treat it like a comedian would—as a sort of gag book. BRENDAN BEHAN, on James Joyce

❋

It is a matter of some embarrassment to me that I have never read Joyce and a dozen other writers who have changed the face of literature. But there you are. I picked up *Ulysses* the other

James Joyce

evening when my eye lit on it, and gave it a go. I stayed with it only for about 20 minutes, then was off and away. It takes more than a genius to keep me reading a book.

E. B. WHITE, on James Joyce

❋

Why don't you write books people can read?

NORA JOYCE, to her husband, James Joyce

❋

My God, what a clumsy *alla putrida* James Joyce is! Nothing but old fags and cabbage-stumps of quotations from the Bible and the rest, stewed in the juice of deliberate, journalistic dirty-mindedness.

D. H. LAWRENCE, on James Joyce

❋

A cruel playful mind like a great soft tiger cat.

WILLIAM BUTLER YEATS, on James Joyce

❋

In Ireland they try to make a cat cleanly by rubbing its nose in its own filth. Mr. Joyce has tried the same treatment on the human subject. I hope it may prove successful.

GEORGE BERNARD SHAW, on James Joyce

I think Joyce and Kafka have said the last word on each of the two forms they developed. There's no one to follow them. They're like cats which have licked the plate clean. You've got to dream up another dish if you're to be a writer.

HENRY GREEN, on James Joyce and Franz Kafka

❀

He couldn't write about sex or value its place in life.

REBECCA WEST, on Franz Kafka

❀

We've lived in a sick world since 1914. It's no accident Kafka has become so popular. He's enjoying the popularity of the prophet whose prophecies have come true. He prophesied the final emergence of the Victim as the archetype of the modern man—the Victim who is slowly teased and tortured and destroyed by forces that are implacable and pitiless and that cannot be understood. IRWIN SHAW, on Franz Kafka

❀

A village explainer, excellent if you were a village, but if you were not, not. GERTRUDE STEIN, on Ezra Pound

I have great admiration for Pound: he is aware of the city, of the well-ordered state, of the long tradition—the enduring ethic. But he doesn't *know*. He hasn't been there. And it shows. Carl Sandburg was one of the few contemporary poets who was able to take the state in his stride. Perhaps he took it in too easy a stride: Edmund Wilson thought so—you remember his contemptuous dismissal. But Carl will have the last word there.

ARCHIBALD MACLEISH, on Ezra Pound and Carl Sandburg

❀

His costume—the velvet jacket and the open-road shirt—was that of the English aesthete of the period. There was a touch of Whistler about him; his language, on the other hand, was Huckleberry Finn's.   SYLVIA BEACH, on Ezra Pound

❀

Ezra detested the "private life," denied that he ever had one, and despised those who were weak enough to need one. He was a warrior who lived on the battlefield, a place of contention and confusion, where a man shows all sides of himself without taking much thought for appearance.

KATHERINE ANNE PORTER, on Ezra Pound

He's teaching me to write, and I'm teaching him to box.

ERNEST HEMINGWAY, on Ezra Pound

❋

Many accepted authors simply do not exist for me. Their names are engraved on empty graves, their books are dummies, they are complete nonentities insofar as my taste in reading is concerned. Brecht, Faulkner, Camus, many others, mean absolutely nothing to me, and I must fight a suspicion of conspiracy against my brain when I see blandly accepted as "great literature" by critics and fellow authors Lady Chatterley's copulations or the pretentious nonsense of Mr. Pound, that total fake. I note he had replaced Dr. Schweitzer in some homes.

VLADIMIR NABOKOV, on Ezra Pound and great literature

❋

Lytton Strachey peered at everyone through thick glasses, looking like an owl in daylight. He is immensely tall, and could be even twice his height if he were not as bent as sloppy asparagus.

CECIL BEATON, on Lytton Strachey

❋

Eliot . . . seemed less alarming than, for example, Lytton Strachey, who could soar far above one with his wit and then follow this up with the depth-charge of one of his famous prolonged silences.

STEPHEN SPENDER, on T. S. Eliot and Lytton Strachey

I know I can write bigger stuff than any man in England.

D. H. LAWRENCE, on himself

✳

I cannot say that I like Lawrence much. He remained too disturbing even when I got to know him well. He had so much need of moral support to take the place of his mother's influence that he kept one—everyone who at all came into contact with him—in a constant state of solicitude. He claimed moral support imperiously—and physical care too.

FORD MADOX FORD, on D. H. Lawrence

✳

If the Christ were content with humble toilers for disciples, that wasn't good enough for our Bert. He wanted dukes' half sisters and belted earls wiping his feet with their hair; grand apotheosis of the snob, to humiliate the objects of his own awe by making them venerate him. In his brisk youth before he met Frieda and became a prophet, he was indeed a confidence man.

ANGELA CARTER, on D. H. Lawrence

✳

Mr. Lawrence looked like a plaster gnome on a stone toadstool in some suburban garden. At the same time he bore some resemblance to a bad self-portrait by Van Gogh. He had a rather matted, dank appearance. He looked as if he had just returned from spending an uncomfortable night in a very dark cave, hiding, perhaps, in the darkness, from something which, at the same time, he on his side was hunting.

EDITH SITWELL, on D. H. Lawrence

❂

Then Edith Sitwell appeared, her nose longer than an ant-eater's, and read some of her absurd stuff.

LYTTON STRACHEY, on Edith Sitwell

❂

I am fairly unrepentant about her poetry. I really think that three quarters of it is gibberish. However, I must crush down these thoughts, otherwise the dove of peace will shit on me.

NOEL COWARD, on Edith Sitwell

❂

So you've been reviewing Edith Sitwell's latest piece of virgin dung, have you? Isn't she a poisonous thing of a woman, lying, concealing, flipping, plagiarising, misquoting, and being as clever a crooked literary publicist as ever.

DYLAN THOMAS, on Edith Sitwell, in a letter to Glyn Jones

❂

Edith—she is a poetess by the way—is a bad loser. When worsted in argument, she throws Queensberry Rules to the winds. She once called me Percy.

[PERCY] WYNDHAM LEWIS, on Edith Sitwell

My sweet La·dy Jane

D.H. Lawrence

Mr. Lewis's pictures appeared . . . to have been painted by a mailed fist in a cotton glove.

EDITH SITWELL, on Wyndham Lewis's artwork

❀

That old pink petulant walrus.

HENRY CHANNON, on Wyndham Lewis

❀

I have been called a Rogue Elephant, a Cannibal Shark, and a crocodile. I am none the worse. I remain a caged, and rather sardonic, Lion in a particularly contemptible and ill-run Zoo.

WYNDHAM LEWIS, on himself

❀

I do not think I have ever seen a nastier-looking man. . . . Under the black hat, when I had first seen them, the eyes had been those of an unsuccessful rapist.

ERNEST HEMINGWAY, on Wyndham Lewis

❀

Enough talent to set up dozens of ordinary writers has been poured into Wyndham Lewis's so-called novels, such as *Tarr* or *Snooty Baronet*. Yet it would be a very heavy labour to read one of these books right through. Some indefinable quality, a sort of literary vitamin . . . is absent from them.

GEORGE ORWELL, on Wyndham Lewis

One day I was told, "Madame Colette [then literary editor of *Le Matin*] would like to see you," and there she was, marvelous to behold in her editorial chair, suddenly addressing me as "Mon petit Sim.'". . . "You know," she said, "I've read your last story, and I ought to have returned it weeks ago. It isn't right. It's almost right. It almost works. But not quite. You are too literary. You must not be literary. Suppress all the literature and it will work. . . ." That was the most useful advice I've ever had in my life, and I owe a grateful candle to Colette for having given it to me.

GEORGES SIMENON, on Colette

❋

I never listen to debates. They are dreadful things indeed. The plain truth is that I am not a fair man, and don't want to hear both sides. On all known subjects, ranging from aviation to xylophone-playing, I have fixed and invariable ideas. They have not changed since I was four or five.

H. L. MENCKEN, on himself

❋

With a pig's eyes that never look up, with a pig's snout that loves muck, with a pig's brain that knows only the sty, and with a pig's squeal that cries only when he is hurt, he sometimes opens his pig's mouth, tusked and ugly, and lets out the voice of God, railing at the whitewash that covers the manure about his habitat.

WILLIAM ALLEN WHITE, on H. L. Mencken

H. L. Mencken suffers from the delusion that he is H. L. Mencken. There is no cure for a disease of that magnitude.

MAXWELL BODENHEIM, on H. L. Mencken

❀

No man in American history has denounced more different people than you have, or in more violent terms, and yet no man that I can recall complains more bitterly when he happens to be hit. Why not stop caterwauling for a while, and try to play the game according to the rules?   H. L. MENCKEN, on Sinclair Lewis

❀

With the publication of *Main Street,* and even more with the publication of *Babbitt,* Lewis became a Successful Author, which meant that he drank heavily, was twice married and twice divorced, and was rude and insulting in public. He once made the mistake of being insulting in public to another author, Theodore Dreiser, who considered this plagiarism.

RICHARD ARMOUR, on Sinclair Lewis

❀

He was a writer who drank, not, as so many have believed, a drunk who wrote.   JAMES LUNDQUIST, on Sinclair Lewis

❀

A dull fellow whose virtue—if there is any—is to be found only in his books.   SINCLAIR LEWIS, on himself

Pale, marmoreal Eliot was there last week, like a chapped office boy on a high stool, with a cold in his head, until he warms a little, which he did. "The critics say I am learned and cold," he said. "The truth is I am neither."

VIRGINIA WOOLF, on T. S. Eliot

❋

I didn't like him one bit. He was a *poseur*. He was married to this woman who was very pretty. My husband [H. G. Wells] and I were asked to see them, and my husband roamed around the flat and there were endless photographs of T. S. Eliot and bits of his poetry done in embroidery by pious American ladies, and only one picture of his wife, and that was when she was getting married. Henry pointed it out to me and said, "I don't think I like that man."

REBECCA WEST, on T. S. Eliot

❋

Rupert had immense charm when he wanted to be charming, and he was inclined to exploit his charm so that he seemed to be sometimes too much the professional charmer. He had a very pronounced streak of hardness, even cruelty, in his character, and his attitude to all other males within a short radius of any attractive female was ridiculously jealous—the attitude of a farmyard cock among the hens.

LEONARD WOOLF, on Rupert Brooke

T.S. Eliot

He is the handsomest man in England, and he wears the most beautiful shirts.

WILLIAM BUTLER YEATS, on Rupert Brooke

❁

It is now quite clear that the fundamental biographic fact about Owen is that he was his mother's boy: his family situation was sufficiently like that of D. H. Lawrence for the comparison to be made.   PHILIP LARKIN, on Wilfred Owen

❁

When I excluded Wilfred Owen [from *The Oxford Book of Modern Verse*], whom I consider unworthy of the poet's corner of a country newspaper, I did not know I was excluding a revered sandwich-board Man of the Revolution, and that some-body has put his worst and most famous poem in a glass-case in the British Museum—however if I had known it, I would have excluded him just the same. He is all blood, dirt and sucked sugar stick.   WILLIAM BUTLER YEATS, on Wilfred Owen

❁

He is at once the truly clever person and the stupid person's idea of the clever person; he is expected to be relentless, to administer intellectual shocks.

ELIZABETH BOWEN, on Aldous Huxley

I don't like his books; even if I admire a sort of desperate courage of repulsion and repudiation in them. But again, I feel only half a man writes the books—a sort of precocious adolescent.

D. H. LAWRENCE, on Aldous Huxley

❋

You were right about Huxley's book [*Ape and Essence*]—it is awful. And do you notice that the more holy he gets, the more his books stink with sex. He cannot get off the subject of flagellating women. GEORGE ORWELL, on Aldous Huxley

❋

He was the tallest English author known to me. He was so tall and thin, so that he seemed to stretch to infinity, that when, long ago, he lived in Hampstead, ribald little boys in that neighborhood used to call out to him: "Cole up there, guv'nor?"

FRANK SWINNERTON, on Aldous Huxley

❋

There appeared a slight sand-headed young man with a handsome clear profile. He wore a formal dark business suit. The moment we were introduced, while we were waiting for the elevator, Bunny gave an accent to the occasion by turning, with a perfectly straight face, a neat somersault.

JOHN DOS PASSOS, on Edmund Wilson

It is so damned easy for such as he, born into easy means, gradu-
ated from a fashionable university into a critical chair overlooking
Washington Square, etc. to sit tight and hatch little squibs of
advice to poets not to be so "professional" as he claims they are.

HART CRANE, on Edmund Wilson

❋

Being, like all those who have worked in Hollywood, a connois-
seur of the damp fart, I place Mr. Wilson high on the list.
His careful and pedestrian and sometimes rather intelligent book
reviews misguide one into thinking there is something in his head
besides mucilage. There isn't.

RAYMOND CHANDLER, on Edmund Wilson

❋

I feel . . . that "love" and the other well-known emotions that
Cummings tirelessly espouses are being imposed on me categori-
cally, and that I stand in some danger of being shot if I do not,
just at that moment, wish to love someone or pick a rose or lean
against a tree watching the snowflakes come down.

JAMES DICKEY, on himself and E. E. Cummings

❋

He was the most brilliant monologuist I have known. What he
poured forth was a mixture of cynical remarks, puns, hyperboles,
outrageous metaphors, inconsequence, and tough-guy talk spoken
from the corner of his wide expressive mouth: pure Cummings, as

if he were rehearsing something that would afterwards appear in print.   MALCOLM COWLEY, on E. E. Cummings

❈

Crane was the archetype of the modern American poet whose fundamental mistake lay in thinking that an irrational surrender of the intellect to the will would be the basis of a new mentality.

ALLEN TATE, on Hart Crane

❈

There were many reasons for his suicide, including his frenzied drinking, his sexual quandary, his lack of money—or prospects of earning it and his feeling that poets had no place in American life, at least during those early years of the Depression. He used to fling up his arms and shout, "What good are poets today! The world needs men of action."

MALCOLM COWLEY, on Hart Crane

❈

Someone told me that when poor Hart finally met his end by jumping overboard from the Havana boat the last his friends on deck saw of him was a cheerful wave of the hand before he sank and drowned. That last friendly wave was very like Hart Crane.

JOHN DOS PASSOS, on Hart Crane

I thought he wrote very well, and I think I liked his writings better than I did him.   JOHN DOS PASSOS, on John Reed

❊

Do you know what my own story is? Well, I was always the poorest boy at a rich man's school. Yes, it was that way at prep schools, and at Princeton, too.

F. SCOTT FITZGERALD, on himself

❊

Aside from his literary genius . . . I think Fitzgerald must have been the worst educated man in the world. . . . He never knew his own strength. . . . When he was a freshman, did the seniors teach him a manly technique of drinking . . . ? If they had it might never have excited him as a vague fatal moral issue.

GLENWAY WESCOTT, on F. Scott Fitzgerald

❊

If Scott had been drinking with us and Mary called us to dinner, Scott'd make it to his feet, all right, but then he'd probably fall down. Alcohol was just poison to him. Because all these guys had these weaknesses, it won them sympathy and favor, more sometimes than a guy without these defects would get.

ERNEST HEMINGWAY, on F. Scott Fitzgerald

I often feel about Fitzgerald that he couldn't distinguish between innocence and social climbing.

> SAUL BELLOW, on F. Scott Fitzgerald

❋

In fact, Mr. Fitzgerald—I believe that is how he spells his name—seems to believe that plagiarism begins at home.

> ZELDA FITZGERALD, in her review of
> F. Scott Fitzgerald's *The Beautiful and Damned*

❋

Sometimes I don't know whether Zelda and I are real or whether we are characters in one of my novels.

> F. SCOTT FITZGERALD, on himself and his wife

❋

It is true that Fitzgerald has been left with a jewel which he doesn't know quite what to do with. For he has been given imagination without intellectual control of it; he has been given the desire for beauty without an aesthetic ideal; and he has been given a gift for expression without very many ideas to express.

> EDMUND WILSON, on F. Scott Fitzgerald

I couldn't read him then and I can't read him now. There was just one passage in a book called *Tender Is the Night*—I read that and thought, "Now I will read this again," because I couldn't be sure. Not only didn't I like his writing, but I didn't like the people he wrote about. I thought they weren't worth thinking about, and I still think so. It seems to me that your human beings have to have some kind of meaning. I just can't be interested in those perfectly stupid meaningless lives.

KATHERINE ANNE PORTER, on F. Scott Fitzgerald

❋

It was terrible about Scott; if you'd seen him you'd have been sick. When he died no one went to the funeral, not a single soul came, or even sent a flower. I said, "Poor son of a bitch," a quote right out of *The Great Gatsby,* and everyone thought it was another wisecrack. But it was said in dead seriousness. Sickening about Scott.

DOROTHY PARKER, on F. Scott Fitzgerald

❋

The ghost of Fitzgerald, dying in Hollywood, with his comeback book unfinished, and his best book, *Tender Is the Night,* scorned—his ghost hangs over every American typewriter.

IRWIN SHAW, on F. Scott Fitzgerald

Perhaps it's just true that Faulkner, if he had been born in, say, Pasadena, might very well still have had that universal quality of mind, but instead of writing *Light in August* he would have gone into television or written universal ads for Jantzen bathing suits.

WILLIAM STYRON, on William Faulkner

❀

For if one thing is more outstanding than another about Mr. Faulkner—some readers find it so outstanding, indeed, that they never get beyond it—it is the uncompromising and almost hypnotic zeal with which he insists on having a style, and, especially of late, the very peculiar style which he insists upon having.

CONRAD AIKEN, on William Faulkner

❀

If this man is a good writer, shrimps whistle Dixie.

CALDER WILLINGHAM, on William Faulkner

❀

I suppose what I like best in Faulkner is the detail. He is a remarkably accurate observer and builds his narratives—which sometimes strike me as turgid—out of the marvelous raw material of what he has seen.

JOHN DOS PASSOS, on William Faulkner

Mr. Faulkner, of course, is interested in making your mind rather than your flesh creep.

CLIFTON FADIMAN, on William Faulkner

❂

Sometimes on a Sunday morning, he used to stroll by a house I occupied in Beverly Hills. I noticed him only because the sight of anybody walking in that environment stamped him as an eccentric, and indeed, it eventually got him into trouble. A prowl car picked him up and he had a rather sticky time of it. The police were convinced he was a finger man for some jewelry mob planning to knock over one of the fancy residences.

S. J. PERELMAN, on William Faulkner

❂

I felt a terrible torment in the man. He always kept his eyes down. We tried to carry on a conversation but he would never participate. Finally he lifted his eyes once to a direct question from me, and the look in his eyes was so terrible, so sad, that I began to cry.

TENNESSEE WILLIAMS, on William Faulkner

Even those who call Mr. Faulkner our greatest literary sadist do not fully appreciate him, for it is not merely his characters who have to run the gauntlet but also his readers.

CLIFTON FADIMAN, on William Faulkner

❀

The final blowup of what was once a remarkable, if minor, talent.

CLIFTON FADIMAN, reviewing Faulkner's
Absalom, Absalom

❀

He has never been known to use a word that might send a reader to the dictionary.

WILLIAM FAULKNER, on Ernest Hemingway

❀

Poor Faulkner. Does he really think big emotions come from big words? ERNEST HEMINGWAY, on William Faulkner

❀

There is no such thing as bad whiskey. Some whiskeys just happen to be better than others. But a man shouldn't fool with booze until he's fifty; then he's a damn fool if he doesn't.

WILLIAM FAULKNER, on himself

Christ, have you ever heard of anyone who drank while he worked? You're thinking of Faulkner. He does sometimes, and I can tell right in the middle of the page when he's had his first one. Besides, who in hell would mix more than one martini at a time, anyway?

> ERNEST HEMINGWAY, on the drinking habits of
> William Faulkner, after being asked by his wife
> if each morning he takes a pitcher of martinis
> to the tower where he writes.

✳

I think of a number of pieces which should be done but that I as a novelist can't or should not do. One would be on the ridiculous occupation of my great contemporaries, and I mean Faulkner and Hemingway, with their own immortality. It is almost as though they were fighting for billing on the tombstone.

> JOHN STEINBECK, on William Faulkner and
> Ernest Hemingway

✳

I have *more* to say than Hemingway, and God knows, I say it *better* than Faulkner.

> CARSON MCCULLERS, on herself,
> Ernest Hemingway, and William Faulkner

Ernest Hemingway

Take Hemingway. People always think that the reason he's easy to read is that he's concise. He isn't. I hate conciseness— it's too difficult. The reason Hemingway is easy to read is that he repeats himself all the time, using "and" for padding.

TOM WOLFE, on Ernest Hemingway

❋

He was very nice when one was alone with him, but the public Hemingway could be troublesome. On one occasion I remember we went into a bar where there were girls. Hemingway immediately took up a guitar and started strumming, being "Hemingway." One of the girls standing with him pointed at me and said, "Tu amigo es muy guapo"—your friend is very handsome. Hemingway became absolutely furious, put down the guitar and left in a rage.

STEPHEN SPENDER, on Ernest Hemingway

❋

The effect upon women is such that they want to go right out and get him and bring him home stuffed.

DOROTHY PARKER, on Ernest Hemingway

He's a great writer. If I didn't think so I wouldn't have tried to kill him. . . . I was the champ and when I read his stuff I knew he had something. So I dropped a heavy glass skylight on his head at a drinking party. But you can't kill the guy. He's not human.   F. SCOTT FITZGERALD, on Ernest Hemingway

❈

Hemingway had the misfortune of being imitated so much that he came to seem like a parody of himself. Besides that, he was a bully. When I was 21 or 22, Nelson Algren published *The Man with the Golden Arm* and Hemingway was quoted on the dust jacket: "All you Capote fans, get your hats and coats and leave the room. Here comes a real writer." I said to myself: Jesus Christ, here's this great guy Hemingway, and he knocks a kid in the head that hard. I would call that pretty bullying.

TRUMAN CAPOTE, on Ernest Hemingway

❈

Hemingway was a jerk.

HAROLD ROBBINS, on Ernest Hemingway

His determination to act out what I might call the least interesting aspects of his own work—the big game hunter and all that. And to do everything that his characters could do and do it well. Always shooting and fishing and all that. I feel that his work suffered from that . . . there's nothing there but the image: Poppa Hemingway.

WILLIAM S. BURROUGHS, on Ernest Hemingway

❀

Hemingway I do not like. I'm not interested in that kind of butch statement. FRAN LEBOWITZ, on Ernest Hemingway

❀

His inclination is toward megalomania and mine toward melancholy.

F. SCOTT FITZGERALD, on Ernest Hemingway and himself

❀

Having just read the admirable profile of Hemingway in the *New Yorker* I realize that I am much too clean to be a genius, much too sober to be a champ, and far, far, too clumsy with a shotgun to live the good life.

RAYMOND CHANDLER, on himself

He can write a scene with an almost suffocating vividness and sense of danger—if he does not add three words too many to make it funny.   JOHN DICKSON CARR, on Raymond Chandler

❁

As a guest, Auden was totally dominating. Breakfast had to be at 8 on the nose, then he expected to be helped with the *Times* crossword puzzle . . . and at 11 he wanted a light snack that the English call elevenses. He always wanted to get back to "mother and home and tea at exactly 4:30." At 6 precisely, he wanted martinis, and if dinner wasn't at exactly 7:30 on the dot, he got very drunk and blamed you for it.

STEPHEN SPENDER, on W. H. Auden

❁

A wedding cake left out in the rain.

STEPHEN SPENDER, commenting on W. H. Auden's face

❁

Mr. Auden's brand of amoralism is only possible if you're the kind of person who is somewhere else when the trigger is pulled.

GEORGE ORWELL, on W. H. Auden

❁

As a poet Nash works under two disadvantages: he is a humorist, and he is easy to understand.

CLIFTON FADIMAN, on Ogden Nash

W.H. Auden

Wodehouse has become not an author but a whole department of a rather delicate art. He is the master of the touchingly inane, of the tears that may be either sympathy with a blundering character or joy over his mishaps, of the ultimate and lordly deadpan.

SINCLAIR LEWIS, on P. G. Wodehouse

❋

When Mr. Wodehouse was led off into captivity by the Germans, he is said to have remarked to a friend "Perhaps after this I shall write a serious book." I wonder. It might be very interesting if he did.

GEORGE ORWELL, on P. G. Wodehouse

❋

With Sean O'Casey's statement that I am "English literature's performing flea," I scarcely know how to deal. Thinking it over, I believe he meant to be complimentary, for all the performing fleas I have met have impressed me with their sterling artistry and their indefinable something which makes the good trouper.

P. G. WODEHOUSE, on himself

❋

Like *The New Yorker* magazine, Mr. Wodehouse is a more dangerous Communist propagandist than twenty *Daily Workers*. For he disposes of the gilded lily and the stuffed bodice not by misunderstanding them and frothing at the mouth, but by understanding them perfectly and smiling till the reader smiles with him, and that, to stuffiness, is deadlier than strychnine.

SINCLAIR LEWIS, on P. G. Wodehouse

❋

Few writers of our time have used words more skillfully, or squandered better talents.

GEORGE ORWELL, on P. G. Wodehouse

❋

We were supposed to be quite good friends, but, you know, in a sort of way I think he was a pretty jealous chap. I think he was probably jealous of all other writers. But I loved his stuff. That's one thing I'm very grateful for: I don't have to like an awful person to like his stuff.

P. G. WODEHOUSE, on A. A. Milne

❋

Tonstant Weader fwowed up.

DOROTHY PARKER, reviewing A. A. Milne's
The House at Pooh Corner

❋

But she was, more than usual, a tangled fishnet of contradictions: she liked the rich because she liked the way they looked, their clothes, the things in their houses, and she disliked them with an open and baiting contempt; she believed in socialism but seldom, except in the sticky sentimental minutes, could stand the sight of a working radical; she drank far too much, spent far too much time with ladies who did, and made fun of them and herself every inch of the way; she faked interest and sympathy with those who bored her and for whom she had no feeling, and yet I never heard her hit mean except where it was, in some sense, justified.

LILLIAN HELLMAN, on Dorothy Parker

❋

Four be the things I'd been better without:
Love, curiosity, freckles and doubt.

DOROTHY PARKER, on herself

❋

She is so odd a blend of Little Nell and Lady Macbeth. It is not so much the familiar phenomenon of a hand of steel in a velvet glove as a lacy sleeve with a bottle of vitriol concealed in its folds.   ALEXANDER WOOLLCOTT, on Dorothy Parker

❋

The affair between Margot Asquith and Margot Asquith will live as one of the prettiest love stories in all literature.

DOROTHY PARKER, reviewing the
autobiography of Margot Asquith

He was like a dry cracker. Brittle.

> EDNA FERBER, on George Kaufman

❋

Miss Ferber, who was fond of wearing tailored suits, showed up at the Round Table one afternoon sporting a new suit similar to one Noel Coward was wearing. "You look almost like a man," Coward said as he greeted her. "So," Miss Ferber replied, "do you."

> ROBERT E. DRENNAN, on Edna Ferber and Noel Coward

❋

I want to be alone on this trip. I don't expect to talk to a man or a woman—just Alex Woollcott.

> EDNA FERBER, on Alexander Woollcott

❋

He looked like something that had gotten loose from Macy's Thanksgiving Day Parade.

> HARPO MARX, on Alexander Woollcott

❋

A Woollcott second edition.

> FRANKLIN PIERCE ADAMS, replying to
> Alexander Woollcott's boast, "What is so rare
> as a Woollcott first edition?"

Old Vitriol and Violets.

> JAMES THURBER, on Alexander Woollcott

❋

No one is so impotent that, meeting Broun face to face, he cannot frighten him into any lie. Any mouse can make this elephant squeal. Yet, I know no more honest being, for, when not threatened, his speech is an innocent emptying of his mind as a woman empties her purse, himself genuinely curious about its contents.

> ALEXANDER WOOLLCOTT, on Heywood Broun

❋

He became mellow before he became ripe.

> ALEXANDER WOOLLCOTT, on Christopher Morley

❋

Robert Benchley has a style that is weak and lies down frequently to rest.

> MAX EASTMAN, on Robert Benchley

❋

You never got very far talking to Benchley about humor. He'd do a take-off on Max Eastman's *Enjoyment of Humor*. "We must understand," he'd say, "that all sentences which begin with W are funny."

> JAMES THURBER, on Robert Benchley

Before Borges we had very few writers who could stand in comparison with the writers of Europe. We have had great writers, but a writer of the universal type, like Borges, is not found very often in our countries. I cannot say that he has been the greatest, and I hope he will be surpassed many times by others, but in every way he has opened the way and attracted attention, the intellectual curiosity of Europe, toward our countries. But for me to fight with Borges because everybody wants me to—I'll never do it. If he thinks like a dinosaur, well, that has nothing to do with my thinking. He understands nothing of what's going on in the contemporary world; he thinks that I understand nothing either. Therefore, we are in agreement.

PABLO NERUDA, on Jorge Luis Borges

❋

Few minds so scientific have deigned to serve the gods of fancy; with his passion for precision and for the complex design, he mounted for display the crudest, most futile lurchings of the human heart—lust, terror, nostalgia. The violence and violent comedy of his novels strikes us, in the main, as merely descriptive, the way the violences of geology are.

JOHN UPDIKE, on Vladimir Nabokov

Jorge Luis Borges

Mr. Nabokov is in the habit of introducing any job of this kind which he undertakes by the announcement that he is unique and incomparable and that everybody else who has attempted it is an oaf and ignoramus, usually with the implication that he is also a low-class person and a ridiculous personality.

EDMUND WILSON, on Vladimir Nabokov

❋

Vladimir Nabokov is surely the most preposterous Transylvanian monster ever to be created by American Academe. He is not a writer at all but a looming beast that stalks the Old Dark House of Campus Literature.

JOHN OSBORNE, on Vladimir Nabokov

❋

Mr. O'Hara's world is populated by the cheap, vulgar, debased and self-destroyed. His reaction to it is a mixture of sardonic scorn, savage contempt and romantic wonder.

ORVILLE PRESCOTT, on John O'Hara

❋

Mr. O'Hara can write like a streak, but he just won't think, or at any rate he won't think in his novels.

CLIFTON FADIMAN, on John O'Hara

Every line of serious work that I have written since 1936 has been written, directly or indirectly, against totalitarianism and for democratic Socialism, as I understand it. It seems to me nonsense, in a period like our own, to think that one can avoid writing of such subjects. Everyone writes of them in one guise or another. It is simply a question of which side one takes and what approach one follows.   GEORGE ORWELL, on himself

❋

He would not blow his nose without moralising on conditions in the handkerchief industry.

CYRIL CONNOLLY, on George Orwell

❋

You remember that Orwell said, when he was answering his own question, why I write, that his leading motive was the desire to be thought clever, to be talked about by people he had never met. I don't think he was being arrogant, I think he was being very honest.   KINGSLEY AMIS, on George Orwell

❋

Now O'Neill is not as good a playwright as, for instance, Albee. I don't think he's even as good as Lanford Wilson. I could give you quite a list. I like O'Neill's writing. He had a great spirit, and a great sense of drama, yet. But most of all it was his spirit, his passion, that moved me. And when *The Iceman Cometh* opened to very bad notices, very mixed notices at best in New York, I wrote him a letter. I said, in reading your play, at first I found it too long, then I gradually realized that its length, and the ponderosity of it, are what gave it a lot of its power. I was deeply moved by it, finally.

TENNESSEE WILLIAMS, on Eugene O'Neill

❋

I think he's a natural playwright. He writes by sanded fingertips.

LILLIAN HELLMAN, on Tennessee Williams

❋

He sometimes ran a purple ribbon through his typewriter and gushed where he should have dammed.

TED KALEM, on Tennessee Williams

❋

[What] makes all Agatha Christie's work commendable, on stage or between covers, is its total incapacity for offending, despite its burden of rage, hate and offensive weapons.

ANTHONY BURGESS, on Agatha Christie

Her slickness in writing has blinded many readers to the fact that her stories, considered as detective stories, are very bad ones. They lack the minimum of probability that even a detective story ought to have, and the crime is always committed in a way that is incredibly tortuous and quite uninteresting.

GEORGE ORWELL, on Dorothy Sayers

❀

Every word she writes is a lie, including *and* and *the*.

MARY MCCARTHY, on Lillian Hellman

❀

If it must be Thomas, let it be Mann, and if it must be Wolfe let it be Nero, but never let it be Thomas Wolfe.

PETER DE VRIES, on Thomas Wolfe

❀

Tom's genius is gigantic, tremendous, immense in its prolific scope but he'll have to learn to cut down, choose, condense.

F. SCOTT FITZGERALD, on Thomas Wolfe

❀

You know Fitzgerald once wrote Thomas Wolfe: "You're a putter-inner and I'm a taker-outer." I stick with Fitzgerald. I don't believe, as Wolfe did, that you have to turn out a massive work before being judged a writer.

JAMES THURBER, on Thomas Wolfe

Writers are forged in injustice as a sword is forged. I wonder if it would make a writer of him, give him the necessary shock to cut the over-flow of words and give him a sense of proportion, if they sent Tom Wolfe to Siberia or to the Dry Tortugas. Maybe it would and maybe it wouldn't.

ERNEST HEMINGWAY, on Thomas Wolfe

❄

I can't read ten pages of Steinbeck without throwing up.

JAMES GOULD COZZENS, on John Steinbeck

❄

Nothing in his books is so dim, insignificantly enough, as the human beings who live in them, and few of them are intensely imagined as human beings at all.

ALFRED KAZIN, on John Steinbeck

❄

The satire of Evelyn Waugh in his early books was derived from his ignorance of life. He found cruel things funny because he did not understand them and he was able to communicate that fun.

CYRIL CONNOLLY, on Evelyn Waugh

I regard writing not as investigation of character but as an exercise in the use of language, and with this I am obsessed. I have no technical psychological interest. It is drama, speech, and events that interest me.   EVELYN WAUGH, on himself

❋

His style has the desperate jauntiness of an orchestra fiddling away for dear life on a sinking ship.

EDMUND WILSON, on Evelyn Waugh

❋

He looked, I decided, like a letter delivered to the wrong address.   MALCOLM MUGGERIDGE, on Evelyn Waugh

❋

I expect you know my friend Evelyn Waugh, who, like you, is a Roman Catholic.

RANDOLPH CHURCHILL, on Evelyn Waugh,
in a remark to the Pope

❋

If I were the Prince of Peace I should choose a less provocative ambassador.   A. E. HOUSMAN, on Bertrand Russell

He is not a favorite of mine. When I went to a Catholic school, I was always adjured to read him, together with Evelyn Waugh and various other Catholic writers, for the salvation of my soul. While it's true that we both have guys in white cassocks staggering around under palm trees, the similarities really do end there.

ROBERT STONE, on Graham Greene

❄

Beckett does not believe in God, though he seems to imply that God has committed an unforgivable sin by not existing.

ANTHONY BURGESS, on Samuel Beckett

❄

Saroyan's peculiarity in insisting that he is a genius is peculiar only in that he does his insisting publicly. Most of the rest of us writers do it in private.

GEORGE JEAN NATHAN, on William Saroyan

❄

The results of American literary elephantiasis can be seen in [such] curiosities as Saul Bellow's reputation.

KINGSLEY AMIS, on Saul Bellow

Dylan Thomas

Dylan wore a green porkpie hat pulled down level with his slightly bulging eyes: like the agate marbles we used as Alley Taws when I was a boy in France, but a darker brown. His full lips were set low in a round full face, a fag-end stuck to the lower one. His nose was bulbous and shiny. He told me afterwards that he used to rub it up with his fist before the mirror every morning until it shone satisfactorily; as a housewife might polish her doorknob or I the silver-topped malacca cane that I affected in those days.

JULIAN MACLAREN-ROSS, on Dylan Thomas

❋

Everybody *loved* him; he was screwing all the coeds in America, drinking all the whiskey, and he'd get up there and read his poems, and then he'd go on and read them somewhere else. He got a lot [of] dough for it. JAMES DICKEY, on Dylan Thomas

❋

In America, visiting British writers are greeted at cocktail parties by faculty wives with "Can you screw as good as Dylan?"

ANTHONY BURGESS, on Dylan Thomas

❋

His passion for lies was congenital: more a practice in invention than a lie. He would tell quite unnecessary ones, which did not in any way improve his situation: such as, when he had been to one cinema, saying it was another, and making up the film that was on: and the obvious ones, that only his mother pretended not to see through, like being carted off the bus into his home, and saying he had been having coffee, in a café, with a friend.

CAITLIN THOMAS, on her husband, Dylan Thomas

❀

A pernicious figure, one who has helped to get Wales and Welsh poetry a bad name . . . and done lasting harm to both.

KINGSLEY AMIS, on Dylan Thomas

❀

I think John Berryman was about the most irritating man I ever saw. But he had this divine discontent—if you want to call it, *terribilitas* is another word the Italians use to describe it—this terrible something. But you see what it did for him—he jumped off a bridge and ended it all.

RICHARD EBERHART, on John Berryman

❀

He was an original poet and a very interesting one, but he wasn't a great poet. That last book *Love and Fame* was a calamity. His publisher should have saved him from it. He shouldn't have published it. I wrote Berryman that it wasn't about love and fame; it was about adolescent lust and notoriety. He never grew up. That was his whole trouble.

ALLEN TATE, on John Berryman

Her first book didn't interest me at all. I was doing my own thing. But after her death, with the appearance of *Ariel*, I think I was influenced, and I don't mind saying it. In a special sort of way, it was daring again. She had dared to do something quite different. She had dared to write hate poems, the one thing I had never dared to write.

ANNE SEXTON, on Sylvia Plath

❊

Randall was the most difficult human being I ever knew. His vanity was astronomical. He insulted everybody. Well, he would sneer at people. He would say, "Oh, how silly." I remember once when he first started reviewing for *The Nation* and *The New Republic* he wrote a long review of Joyce Kilmer. I said, "why did you do that? It's like flogging a dead donkey." He couldn't resist it. He tore old Kilmer's corpse all to pieces.

ALLEN TATE, on Randall Jarrell and Joyce Kilmer

❊

He was bearded, formidable, bristling, with a high-pitched nervous voice and the wariness of a porcupine.

STANLEY KUNITZ, on Randall Jarrell

❊

He is a bad novelist and a fool. The combination usually makes for great popularity in the U.S.

GORE VIDAL, on Alexander Solzhenitsyn

He's a second-rate Stephen Birmingham. And Stephen Birmingham is third-rate.

TRUMAN CAPOTE, on Louis Auchincloss

❀

I suppose my central theme is the theme of spiritual isolation. Certainly I have always felt alone.

CARSON MCCULLERS, on herself

❀

Unlike too many other "legends," she was as real as her face.

GORE VIDAL, on Carson McCullers

❀

Or you can disappear like Salinger, whose doom I lay squarely at the door of the *New Yorker* magazine for paying him the retainer. There are some people who flourish on being paid retainers because it stops them worrying about how they're going to pay for the groceries next week. Very few, however. I think most people need a little pressure like that.

KINGSLEY AMIS, on J. D. Salinger

I don't like Salinger, not at all. That last thing isn't a novel anyway, whatever it is. I don't like it. Not at all. It suffers from this terrible sort of metropolitan sentimentality and it's so narcissistic. And to me, also, it seemed so false, so calculated. Combining the plain man with an absolutely megalomaniac egoism. I simply can't stand it.

MARY MCCARTHY, on J. D. Salinger

❁

The greatest mind ever to stay in prep school.

NORMAN MAILER, on J. D. Salinger

❁

I think it's really important to stay in journalism. Otherwise you run the danger of getting as completely out of touch as Salinger. What I would have Salinger do is write four pieces of journalism right now because it would force him to get in touch.

TOM WOLFE, on J. D. Salinger

❁

For a while people would bring me messages from him. He would send his love. I never took it too seriously, because there is now something Italian about Jones. He only sends his love to people he has decided to kill.

NORMAN MAILER, on James Jones

A hustler who comes on like Job.

ISHMAEL REED, on James Baldwin

❋

Ellison is as angry as anybody can be and still live.

JAMES BALDWIN, on Ralph Ellison

❋

Not since the Marquis de Sade has so much mechanical copulation been so gravely arranged.

JOHN UPDIKE, on William S. Burroughs's *Port of Saints*

❋

[He resembles] a Vermont farmer who had been married to his wife for sixty years, and the day she dies someone says, "I guess you're going to miss her a lot, Zeke," and he says, "No, never did get to like her much."

NORMAN MAILER, on William S. Burroughs

❋

I remember an encounter between the people in the bus and Jack Kerouac, somewhere on Madison Avenue. Neal Cassady was driving the bus, and Kerouac, Ginsberg, the Orlovskys, and a couple of other people, including a guy who claimed to be Terry Southern and wasn't, were in this party. Kerouac had reached the stage of being very alcoholic and embittered—boy, he hated us. He was jealous that Ken Kesey had grabbed Neal as a bus driver. These people were just a bunch of California hippies. He did not see us as angels, seraphs, and all the terrific things that he saw his own generation as. It's true, in a way we were the opposite—we were a lot healthier and California-like; we were just not a New York number. There was a lot of the hayseed, cowboy element in Kesey that clashed with the Eighth Street commando—an East/West Coast cultural clash of ages.

ROBERT STONE, on Jack Kerouac and Ken Kesey

❋

His rhythms are erratic, his sense of character is nil, and he is as pretentious as a rich whore, as sentimental as a lollipop. Yet I think he has a large talent.

NORMAN MAILER, on Jack Kerouac

❋

Allen Ginsberg asked me when he was 19-years-old, should I change my name to Allen Renard? You change your name to Allen Renard I'll kick you right in the balls! Stick to Ginsberg . . . and he did. That's one thing I like about Allen.

JACK KEROUAC, on Allen Ginsberg

❋

That's not writing—that's typing.

TRUMAN CAPOTE, on Jack Kerouac

Truman Capote has made lying an art. A minor art.

GORE VIDAL, on Truman Capote

❀

I'm about as tall as a shotgun, and just as noisy. I think I have rather heated eyes. . . . I have a very sassy voice. I like my nose. . . . Do you want to know the real reason I push my hair down over my forehead? Because I have two cowlicks. If I didn't push my hair forward, it would make me look as though I had two feathery horns.   TRUMAN CAPOTE, on himself

❀

In those days Truman was about the best companion you could want. He had not turned bitchy. Well, he had not turned *maliciously* bitchy. He was full of fantasies and mischief.

TENNESSEE WILLIAMS, on Truman Capote

❀

Truman Capote I do not know well, but I like him. He is as tart as a grand aunt, but in his way he is a ballsy little guy, and he is the most perfect writer of my generation; he writes the best sentences word for word, rhythm upon rhythm.

NORMAN MAILER, on Truman Capote

What is Mailer? A romantic who wants to be what he is not, a tall blond handsome, a ruthless goy like Sergius. Mailer is closest in temperament to Scott Fitzgerald.

GORE VIDAL, on Norman Mailer

❋

Chandler Brossard is a mean, pricky guy who's been around, and he'd have been happier as a surgeon than a novelist, but he is original, and parts I read of *The Bold Saboteurs* were sufficiently interesting for me to put the book away—it was a little too close to some of my own notions.

NORMAN MAILER, on Chandler Brossard

❋

It may well be that I'm "mean and pricky," but how did he find out? I did not see that much of him, and I thought that I was just as sweet as a little church mouse the times we did meet. But there you are. Maybe he just heard it from an itinerant malcontent.   CHANDLER BROSSARD, on Norman Mailer

❋

I have a confession to make. I have nothing to say about any of the talented women who write today. Out of what is no doubt a fault in me, I do not seem to be able to read them. . . . At the risk of making a dozen devoted enemies for life, I can only say the sniffs I get from the ink of the women are always fey, old-hat, Quainstsy, Goysy, tiny, too dykily psychotic, crippled, creep-

Norman Mailer

ish, fashionable, frigid. . . . The little I have read of Herbert Gold reminds me of nothing so much as a woman writer.

NORMAN MAILER, on Herbert Gold

❀

Poor Norman, he yells so loud because he's deaf. I don't think it makes sense to try and outyell him. We were unfriends around Manhattan while I was living there, though I didn't dislike him, just thought him sad. Now he's found a way to make the scene without doing the usual hard work of thinking and writing. Well, let him make it his way. I don't like the noise.

HERBERT GOLD, on Norman Mailer

❀

Herbert Gold used to be a mosquito. Now he is an angry mosquito. I better get my ass covered.

NORMAN MAILER, on Herbert Gold

❀

I was smashed, too much so to recall who else was there apart from Norman Mailer, of course, who was not stabbing anyone at the time, and who either then or on a later occasion seemed to be offering me friendship, which I instinctively evaded.

KINGSLEY AMIS, on Norman Mailer

I have demonstrated that, at least in his dealings with me, Vidal has proved contemptible, a dogged liar, a foul human being.

WILLIAM F. BUCKLEY, on Gore Vidal

❋

Yes, well, it may be laziness, but on the rare occasions when I do pick up Vidal, whose early books I enjoyed before he was celebrated as he is now, he seems to me to suffer from American cleverness: the fear of being thought stupid, or dull, or behind the times. I think that's a very bad attitude for the novelist to adopt. He must not mind being thought boring and pompous from time to time—let's hope he avoids it, but if he runs too far in the opposite direction, he's heading for disaster.

KINGSLEY AMIS, on Gore Vidal

❋

We've both employed an episodic structure, and once in a while our ideas dovetail, but I'm obsessed with the poetics of prose and he is clearly not, I'm optimistic and he's pessimistic, I'm complex and he's simple: His sensibility is much more middle-aged and middle-class.

TOM ROBBINS, on Kurt Vonnegut

So many young writers I've met are uneducated. They don't read. They don't read what started things . . . produced the trends. They don't know the classics. If they become enthusiastic, it's about someone like Kurt Vonnegut, who is uncopyable. If they try to copy him, they're in for disaster.

IRWIN SHAW, on Kurt Vonnegut

❂

He has a very fragrant if slightly redolent breath; but so far as I know a dangerous idea has never entered his brain. His mind is happy as a virgin oyster. Oysters taste wonderful if you like them, but they stir no foundations.

NORMAN MAILER, on William Styron

❂

I think Bill Styron is very good, but then everybody says that. Just as everyone has a token Jew or a token homosexual, Styron is everybody's favorite good writer.

TRUMAN CAPOTE, on William Styron

❂

For example, John Updike for years has been criticized as a man of no substance, as a man who "writes well." The criticism of Updike's novels is that they are written well. That's absurd.

STANLEY ELKIN, on John Updike

Now a novelist who I admire most in this country is Philip Roth. He's a fabulous writer. The guy's terrific. He's the closest thing we have to Dickens.

>   TOM WOLFE, on Philip Roth

✸

Philip Roth is a good writer, but I wouldn't want to shake hands with him.

>   JACQUELINE SUSANN, reacting to Philip Roth's
>   novel *Portnoy's Complaint*

✸

She looks like a truck driver in drag.

>   TRUMAN CAPOTE, on Jacqueline Susann

✸

For the reader who has put away comic books, but isn't ready yet for editorials in the *Daily News*.

>   GLORIA STEINEM, on Jacqueline Susann

✸

I didn't think I was going to be a woman writer. Nor did I have a woman model. My models when I was in my early teens were Gide, Mann, Kafka. I never thought: There are women writers, so this is something I can be. I thought: There are writers; this is something I want to be. I learned to read very early, and

Philip Roth

the very first writers who enthralled me were Edgar Allen Poe,
Jack London, Victor Hugo, and then the Brontës.

SUSAN SONTAG, on herself

❄

I once said that if there were a particular woman writer today in
America who could compare to Hemingway, it'd probably be
Joan Didion. She has that same sense of the power of the sentence sitting by itself and the power of the next sentence. There's
no accident that she writes movies and lives with film because her
work, like Hemingway's, is montage. That is, there's an
assumption that the reader's going to pay enough attention to each
sentence so they'll feel the next sentence come into place. It's
very much like cuts in a film.

NORMAN MAILER, on Joan Didion

❄

I'm no Joan Didion—there are no intelligent, unhappy people in
my books. I want to be known as a writer of good, entertaining
narrative. I'm not trying to be taken seriously by the East Coast
literary establishment. But I'm taken very seriously by the
bankers.   JUDITH KRANTZ, on herself and Joan Didion

❄

As a work of art it has the same status as a long conversation
between two not very bright drunks.

CLIVE JAMES, on Judith Krantz's *Princess Daisy*

Judith Krantz

She's another no-talent. . . . Usually pornography is written by men. . . . Well, she looks sort of like a man, in drag. . . . But don't say that, 'cause she's a nice enough person.

JAMES DICKEY, on Erica Jong

❋

His humor is the humor of the mob against the victim, of sword against the pen, of six sleazeballs on a street-corner in Bensonhurst yelling at passing cars. P. J. O'Rourke is precisely the kind of ignorant pinheaded loudmouth political pimp Mencken boned and gutted for breakfast. He's Babbitt with attitude.

TONY HENDRA, on P. J. O'Rourke

❋

Sheldon is a graduate of "The Terrible Secret" School of Fiction Writing, in which most of his characters hide huge chunks of their past from each other so we'll keep the pages turning. Protagonists also spend endless hours harboring a horrible legacy or painful lie, only to find that personal catastrophe may often lead to romance, riches, and the possibility of a sequel.

PATRICIA HOLT, on Sidney Sheldon

❋

Anyone who commits to a large historical novel has to know how to plot, tell a story. Michener can bore a guy to death, though you can get a damn good history lesson.

LEON URIS, on James Michener

I admire John Le Carré. And I honestly can't say about Robert Ludlum, because I haven't read one of his books. They're too big for me to start. I don't like starting on big books.

DICK FRANCIS, on John Le Carré and Robert Ludlum

❋

You can read just a few pages of Stephen King and see that he's a very sensuous writer. It's the way he perceives the world: how a screen door closing sounds, or the flavor of a chocolate bar or a hamburger or whatever—it's all in there.

ANNE RICE, on Stephen King

❋

Stephen King finds at the center of horror fiction, rationale grounds, compulsion to hope.

ANDREW GREELEY, on Stephen King

❋

People want to know why I do this, why I write such gross stuff. I like to tell them I have the heart of a small boy—and I keep it in a jar on my desk.   STEPHEN KING, on himself

Italics indicate pages with illustrations.